Theatre Accord in association with Tara Arts

PARADISE
OF THE
ASSASSINS

Written and directed by Anthony Clark

Based on the book by Abdul Halim Sharar

Premiered on Thursday 15 September 2016 at Tara Theatre

THEATRE ACCORD

Theatre Accord explores diversity in the contemporary world through drama that is vibrant and resonant. It was founded by director/writer Anthony Clark in 2014 to work in partnership with companies who share Theatre Accord's ethos.

As well as freelancing with numerous companies including, Tara Arts, RSC and NT, Anthony Clark was Artistic Director of Contact Theatre, Associate Artistic Director of Birmingham Rep (founder of the Door) and Artistic Director of Hampstead Theatre.

Anthony has written for RSC, NT and many of this country's most prestigious repertory companies.

www.anthonyclarktheatre.com

theatreaccord@gmail.com

Tara Arts are one of the UK's foremost creators of cross-cultural theatre. Their work consistently seeks to connect worlds, through new writing and reimagined classics. The company was founded in 1977 by Artistic Director Jatinder Verma, and will celebrate its 40th anniversary in 2017.

The new Tara Theatre, which this production opens, will be the country's first dedicated small-scale multicultural theatre, housing a 100-seat auditorium and a separate rehearsal/development Studio, along with an outdoor patio space.

Architecturally, the new Tara Theatre is a fusion of Edwardian brick and Indian wood, including doors and architraves from India, all held together within a 21st century steel cube. The architectural multiculturalism of the building will be echoed in the artistic programme on offer.

Tara Arts is a registered charity no: 295547

Tara-arts.com | @Tara_Arts

Theatre Accord in association with Tara Arts

PARADISE
OF THE
ASSASSINS

Written and directed by Anthony Clark

Based on a novel by Abdul Halim Sharar

Designed by Matilde Marangoni

Original music by Danyal Dhondy

Lighting designed by Amy Mae

Thurs 15 Sept – Sat 8 October	Thurs 13 – Sat 15 October
Tara Theatre	Belgrade Theatre
356 Garratt Lane, London, SW18 4ES	Belgrade Square, Coventry, CV1 1GS
Box Office: 020 8333 4457	Box Office: 024 7655 3055
www.tara-arts.com	www.belgrade.co.uk

CAST BIOGRAPHIES

In Alphabetical Order

Ralph Birtwell – MUSTAFA, KAZIM, MASTER OF THE CAVE

Training: LAMDA

For Tara Arts: *Macbeth*

Theatre: includes *Romeo & Juliet*, *Richard III*, *The Relapse* (Royal Shakespeare Company); *The Royal Hunt Of The Sun*, *Market Boy*, *The Man of Mode* (National Theatre); *A Midsummer Night's Dream*; *East Is East* (Leicester Haymarket); *Macbeth* (Tara Arts); *Sleeping Beauty*, *Aladdin* (Theatre Royal Stratford-East); *Ali Baba And The 40 Thieves* (The Theatre, Chipping Norton); *Bombay Dreams* (Apollo Victoria); *Jesus Christ Superstar* (UK/European Tour); *The Far Pavilions* (Shaftesbury Theatre); *The Witches Of Eastwick* (UK Tour); *Call Me Madam* (Union Theatre); *Joseph & The Amazing Technicolor Dreamcoat* (Madinat Dubai); *Aspire* (The Dome Sports St Qatar); *I Was Looking At The Ceiling And Then I Saw The Sky* (Southwark Playhouse); *Tamburlaine* (ON); *Half N Half* (Weston Studio, WMC); *Bend It Like Beckham* (Workshop)

and *A Subject Of Scandal & Concern* (Finborough Theatre).

Television & Film: includes *East Is East*; *Coronation Street*; *Harley Street*; *Law & Order*; *Crisis Command*; *Doctors*; *The Vice*; *The Cops*; *Clocking Off*; *Blood Strangers*; *Tales From Pleasure Beach*; *Shooting Stars* and numerous commercials.

Rina Fatania – PARISA, PRINCESS

Training: Central School of Speech and Drama

Theatre: includes *Love N Stuff* (Theatre Royal Stratford East, 2013 & 2016); *Dead Dog in a Suitcase* (Kneehigh Theatre Company UK & International tour); *Mummyji Presents* (Birmingham Rep – The Door); *Aladdin* (De Montford Hall, Leicester); *The Empress* (RSC, The Swan Theatre); *Dick Whittington* (Hackney Empire); *Wah! Wah! Girls* (Sadler's Wells/ UK Tour); *Cinderella* (Hackney Empire); *Guantanamo Boy* (Brolly Productions); *Britain's Got Bhangra* (UK Tour); *The Vagina Monologues* (Alchemy Festival, Southbank); *The House of Bilquis Bibi* (Hampstead Theatre & UK Tour); *Britain's Got Bhangra* (Rifco Arts); *Wuthering Heights* (Tamasha Theatre

Co.); *It Aint All Bollywood* (Rifco Arts/ National & Pakistan Tour); *A Fine Balance* (Tamasha Theatre Co.); *The Child of Divide* (Tamasha Theatre Co/ New York & L.A Tour); *Meri Christmas* (Rifco Arts); *The Deranged Marriage* (Rifco Arts); *Strictly Dandia* (Tamasha Theatre Co.); *Bombay Dreams* (Apollo Victoria, West End) and *Arabian Nights* (Midland Arts Centre).

Film: includes *Raabta* (Bollywood Film); *Digital-Mummji Presents* (Character devised by Rina Fatania) (BBC Space/ Pravesh Kumar); *Mumbai Charlie* (Pukkanasha Films) and *The Travel Londoner* (Painting Pictures).

Radio: includes *We Are Water* (BBC World Service); *Oceans Unite Us* (BBC World Service), *Silver Street* (BBC Asian Network) and *Baby Farming* (BBC Radio 3).

Music Video: Mother, MC Soecial-Sanuvi (Cre8 Media), Wife, Kolaveri Di, Solo Productions.

Skye Hallam – ZAMURRUD

Training: RADA

Theatre: includes *Agamemnon, Troilus and Cressida, The Provok'd Wife, Othello, Dying For It, In Arabia We'd All Be, Kings* and *Kindertransport* (RADA).

Film: includes *Box 8275* and *The Ness* (RADA).

Radio: includes *The Wall, Dombey and Son* and *Alice's Wunderland* (RADA).

Asif Khan – HUSSAIN

Training: RADA

Asif trained at The Royal Academy Of Dramatic Art (RADA), where he won a Laurence Olivier Bursary Award.

Theatre: includes *Love, Bombs & Apples* (Arcola & UK Tour 2016); *Handbagged* (UK Tour 2015, Tricycle Theatre/Eleanor Lloyd Productions); *Love, Bombs & Apples* (Arcola Theatre 2015); *Punjabi Boy* (RichMix); *Multitudes* (Tricycle Theatre); *The Nutcracker & The Mouse King* (Unicorn Theatre); *The Book* (Flying Cloud); *Queen of the Nile* (Hull Truck); *Kabaddi Kabaddi Kabaddi* (Arcola Theatre); *The Snow Queen* (Unicorn Theatre/ Trestle) and in *Snookered* (Tamasha/ Bush Theatre), which was nominated for 'Best New Play' & 'Best Ensemble Cast' by Off West End Theatre Awards 2012, and won 'Best New Play' at the Manchester Theatre Awards. Also: *Mixed Up North* (Out of Joint); *Twelfth Night* (National Theatre); *Playback* (Ankur Productions); and *Three Sisters,*

Rookery Nook, The Last Days of Judas Iscariot (Toby Frow) and *Julius Caesar, Antigone, The Glass Menagerie* at RADA.

Television & Film: *Love Type D* (Feature film to be released in 2016); *Spooks* (Series 10); *The Dumping Ground, Doctors, Casualty* (BBC). *Dark Matters, Terry Pratchett's Going Postal* (Sky1); *Man Down* & *Bradford Riots* (Channel 4) and *The Plot to Bring Down Britain›s Planes* (BAFTA Winner).

He was recently nominated for The Male Actor of the Year Award at the BEAM Awards 2016.

Naveed Khan – ALI VUJOODI
Training: The Oxford School of Drama.

Theatre: includes *Darknet* (Southwark Playhouse); *Pitcairn* (The Globe/Out of Joint); *Pioneer* (Curious Directive and Watford Palace Theatre); *The Waiting Game* (Kazzum Arts); *59 Minutes to Save Christmas* (Slung Low with The Barbican 2013 and Sheffield Crucible 2015); *These Bones of Mine* (Curious Directive); *After The Rainfall* (Curious Directive); *The Truth Teller* (The King's Head); *The Tagore Project* (The West Yorkshire Playhouse); *The*

Trial (Watford Palace Theatre); *Lincoln Road* (Eastern Angles) and *Jerusalem* (The Oxford Playhouse). Theatre credits in training include *Plasticine* (The Southwark Playhouse) and *A Midsummer Night's Dream* (Blenheim Palace Open-Air).

Television: includes *Josh* (BBC3); *Birds of a Feather, Catherine Tate – Nan Specials* and *River*.

Film: includes *Second Coming* (directed by Debbie Tucker Green) and *Survivor* (directed by James McTeigue).

Karl Seth – KHURSHAH
Training: LAMDA

Theatre: includes *Taming of the Shrew, Dick Whittington* (Mercury Theatre);*The Firebird* (Polka Children's Theatre); *Julius Caesar* (Palace, Manchester and National tour); *All on a Summer's Day* (Regent's Park Open Air); *Mixed Blessings*(Palace, Westcliffe-on- Sea); *The Flood* (Rochdale); *Hiawatha* (Crucible, Sheffield); *Elidor* (Contact); *Beauty and the Beast* (Rochdale); *The Jungle Book* (Library, Manchester); *The Bottle Imp* (Major Road Theatre and National tour); *The King and I* (BOC Covent Garden Festival); *The*

Snow Queen (Theatre Clwyd); *East is East* (Trafalgar Studios) and *Bend It Like Beckham* (Phoenix Theatre).

Television & Film: Includes *Jobs for the Boys*; *Merseybeat*; *Young Indiana Jones Chronicles*; *The Piglet Files* and *Four Lions*.

Mitesh Soni – MUSA, IMAM, DEEDAR

Training: Guildford School of Acting

For Tara Arts: *Macbeth*

Theatre: includes *Coming Up* (Watford Palace); *Romeo & Juliet* (National Theatre);*The Good Person of Sichuan* (Colchester); *Arabian Nights* (Manchester Library Theatre); *This Place Means* (Greenwich); *The Firework Maker's Daughter* (Theatre by the Lake, Keswick); *The Rise & Fall of Little Voice* (Dukes, Lancaster); *Peter Pan* (New Vic Stoke); *Rafta Rafta* (Bolton Octagon/ New Vic Stoke); *The Jungle Book* (Birmingham Stage Company UK Tour); *Cloud Pictures* (Polka Theatre); *Mercury Fur* (Goldsmiths); *Lord of the Flies* (Pilot Theatre UK tour); *Meteorite* (Hampstead Theatre); *Cloud 9* (Queen Mother Theatre) and *Blood Wedding* (Edinburgh Festival).

Television: includes *The Agency, Run, Threesome* and *The Canterbury Tales*

Film: includes *Rise of The Footsoldier*

2, Syriana, Ghost of Life, Nine Lives London, Alpha Mayall and *Lost Night.*

Awards: 2012 Manchester Theatre Award- Best Ensemble – *Arabian Nights*

Tripti Tripuraneni – MARJAN

Training: Tripti recently graduated from the Guildhall school of Music and Drama and is very excited to be making her professional debut with *Paradise of the Assassins.*

Theatre: whilst training include *On the Twentieth Century, Top Girls, Lulu, The Secret Rapture, Richard II, Trojan Women, Into The Woods, Habeas Corpus, Separate Tables, Love for Love* and *Marine Parade.*

CREATIVE TEAM BIOGRAPHIES

Abdul Halim Sharar - Author of the novel *Paradise of Assassins*

Abdul Halim Sharar was a progressive writer in Urdu in late 19th century India. Born in Lucknow just after the 1857 Mutiny against the British, he developed his writing career by serving as a correspondent for the Oudh Akhbar- an immensely popular Urdu weekly. It was here that he employed the format of a serialised novel as a literary vehicle. His view of the novel as a means of exploring a larger historical sense of mission remains a characterised feature of the Urdu novel down to the modern era.

He was a prolific writer of more than a hundred books, plays and essays. His famous novels include *Malikul Azia Varjina* (1889); *Paradise of the Assassins* (1899) and *Fateh Maftuh* (1916). Abdul Halim Sharar died in 1926, having completed a 3 volume history of Islam on commission from Nizam of Hyderabad.

Anthony Clark – Writer/Director

Anthony Clark read Drama at Manchester University. He followed a BA Hons Degree with a post graduate Diploma in Playwriting. He is currently working as freelance director, playwright and teacher having previously been Artistic Director of Hampstead Theatre (2003-10), Associate Artistic Director Birmingham Rep (1997-2002), Associate Director Birmingham Rep (1990-97), Artistic Director Contact Theatre (1984-90) and Assistant Director Orange Tree (1981-83). He has freelanced extensively working with companies that include The National, RSC, Young Vic, Bristol Old Vic Leicester Haymarket, Nottingham Playhouse, Tara Arts. Several of plays have been published and produced throughout Britain and internationally. These include *Wake*, and *The Power of Darkness* (1983) for the Orange Tree, *Tide Mark* for RSC (1984) *Green* for Contact Theatre (1985), *Our Brother David* (2012) for Watford Palace, and children's adaptations of *The Little Prince* and *The Red Balloon* (National Theatre).

Matilde Marangoni – Designer

Matilde Marangoni trained on the MA Performance Design and Practice course at Central Saint Martins (London), graduating with a first class degree. She had previously studied on the BA Theatre Design course at Accademia di Belle Arti di Brera (Milan), and gained further experience in theatre as a set and costume designer. Her passion for theatre strengthened throughout the time at Central Saint Martins, where she explored various forms of performance and experimented with creative and thoughtful approaches to design. Her work crosses a range of genres: theatre, film, installations, events and exhibitions. Since graduating, she has been shortlisted as one of the twelve finalists of the Linbury Prize for Stage Design 2015 and awarded the National Theatre Linbury bursary (2017). Some of her mentionable projects include the theatre pieces *Here and Gone* (Clifftown Theatre, 2016) and *Shaw's Women* (Tristan Bates Theatre, 2015), the immersive site specific performances *Nova Insula* (Inteatro Marche, 2015) and *(Uns) table* (Platform Theatre, 2015), and the interactive installation *Mnemonic* (All Hallows Church, 2014). She has worked as an assistant designer on a range of projects including *Orpheus and Eurydice* (Platform Theatre, 2013), *Toynbee* (Toynbee Studios, 2013), *Romeo and Juliet* (Ovalhouse, 2012), *Nine Rooms* (Old Vic Tunnels, 2012), *Hexenjagd* (Schauspielhaus Graz, 2011), and *Esequie Solenni* (Teatro Franco Parenti, 2011).

Danyal Dhondy – Composer

Danyal Dhondy is a composer from South London. Since graduating from Cambridge University with a degree in Music in 2008, he has worked extensively in the fields of opera and theatre music. Most recently, he was commissioned by Musica Europa to write a Children's opera, *Das Schlossgespenst,* and scored a new play by Theatre6, *Honest.* He is currently working on an orchestral piece, a ballet, and a new opera on the subject of *1001 Nights.* Having regularly worked at Tara's old theatre, he is delighted to be involved in its first post-renovation production. A selection of his music can be heard at www.danyaldhondy.com.

Amy Mae – Lighting Designer

Amy works across Theatre, Dance, Site Specific and Devised performance.

Amy trained at RADA on the postgraduate Stage Electrics and Lighting Design course and has a degree in Stage Management and Performing Arts from the University of Winchester.

She won the Knight of Illumination Award in 2016 in the musicals category for Sweeney Todd.

Recent Credits include: *The Lounge* (China Plate and Inspector Sands, UK Tour); *Knife Edge* (Pond Restaurant, Dalston); *Minaturists 55* (Arcola Theatre); *Prize Fights* (Royal Academy of Dramatic Art); *Orphans* (Southwark Playhouse); *Macbeth* (Italia Conti); *I'm Not Here Right Now* (Paines Plough's Roundabout and Soho Theatre); *Liola* (New Diorama Theatre); *Children In Uniform* (Tristan Bates Theatre); *Punk Rock* (Tristan Bates Theatre); *Sweeney Todd* (Harringtons Pie and Mash Shop and West End); *The Three Sisters* (Cockpit Theatre); *Cat Couture* (Music Video); *In Bed* (London Theatre Workshop); *Henry V* (Royal Academy of Dramatic Art); *Pool, The Gut Girls* (Brockley Jack Theatre) and *The Legacy* (The Place).

Programming Credits Include: *Tannhauser* (Longborough Festival Opera); *Robin Hood* (Stratford East Theatre Royal); *Lela & Co* (The Royal Court); *Dirty Butterfly* (The Young Vic) and *Red Forest* (The Young Vic).

Re-lighting Credits Include: *White Christmas* (Pitlochry Festival Theatre).

Production Team
Production Manager: Ned Lay
Company Stage Manager:
Emily Moitoi-Sturman
Deputy Stage Manager:
Kirsty MacDiarmid
Costume Supervisor: Alison Cartledge

For Tara Arts
Artistic Director: Jatinder Verma
Executive Producer: Jonathan Kennedy
Associate Director: Claudia Mayer
General Manager: Alexandra Wyatt
Marketing Manager: Emma Martin
Technical & Operations Manager: Tom
Kingdon
Development Associate:
Frances Mayhew
Finance Manager: Xiao Hong (Sharon)
Zhang
Finance Officer: Julie Quan
PR: Elin Morgan, Mobius

Supported using public funding by
ARTS COUNCIL ENGLAND
LOTTERY FUNDED

PARADISE OF THE ASSASSINS

Anthony Clark

PARADISE OF THE ASSASSINS

based on a story by Abdul Halim Sharar

OBERON BOOKS
LONDON

WWW.OBERONBOOKS.COM

First published in 2016 by Oberon Books Ltd
521 Caledonian Road, London N7 9RH
Tel: +44 (0) 20 7607 3637 / Fax: +44 (0) 20 7607 3629
e-mail: info@oberonbooks.com
www.oberonbooks.com

A catalogue record for this book is available from the British
Library.

PB ISBN: 9781786820334
E ISBN: 9781786820341

Cover design by feastcreative.com

Printed and bound by CPI Group (UK) Ltd, Croydon, CR0 4YY.

Visit www.oberonbooks.com to read more about all our books
and to buy them. You will also find features, author interviews and
news of any author events, and you can sign up for e-newsletters
so that you're always first to hear about our new releases.

For Jatinder Verma

Characters

HUSSAIN
a young Sunni nobleman from the town of Aamil

ZAMURRUD
a young Sunni noblewoman from the same town

SHEIKH ALI VUJOODI
a member of the inner circle of the Batiniyah Sect

IMAM NAJAMUDDIN NAISHAPURI
a religious scholar and teacher. Hussain's Uncle

KAZIM JUNOOBI
a mendicant monk, beggar.

MASTER OF THE CAVE
a member of the inner circle of the Batiniyah Sect

IMAM QAYEM QAYAMAT

(THE KHURSHAH)
ruler of the castle of Alamut, and Imam of all Batiniyah

DEEDAR
disciple who killed the Mongol Chughtai Khan

BALGHAN KHATOON
Chughtai Khan's daughter. Mongol Princess

MARJAN
a houri

PARISA
a houri

MUSTAFA

A eunuch guard

MONGOL SOLDIERS

MEN IN PARADISE

PUPILS OF IMAM NAJAMUDDIN NAISHAPURI

BATINIYAH RECRUITS

ATTENDANTS

PASSERSBY

HOURIS

Company and Staging

A versatile ensemble, of no less than eight actors, play a range
of characters, and should devise the staging, music and sound
effects as far as possible, themselves.

Titles

The title of each scene should either be spoken, presented on a
placard, or projected at the start of each scene.

A/ marks the point of interruption in
overlapping dialogue.

SCENE ONE

Winter in the 650th year of Hejirah – 1252. HUSSAIN and ZAMURRUD are doing Hajj – a pilgrimage to the sacred house of Allah. In the shadow of the Alburz mountains – in present-day Iran – they come to a fork in the road and disagree about which route to take.

The sound of a biting wind. ZAMURRUD walks slowly into view followed by HUSSAIN. She stops, he passes her. To protect them from the cold, both wear layers of clothes. They look like a couple of mullahs. HUSSAIN stops and turns to her.

HUSSAIN: Tired?

ZAMURRUD: What day is it?

HUSSAIN: Today?

> *Beat.*

> Thursday.

ZAMURRUD: Thursday ?

HUSSAIN: Eight days on the road and no one's come looking for us.

ZAMURRUD: I'm not tired.

HUSSAIN: Cold?

ZAMURRUD: I know what they're thinking.

HUSSAIN: *(Mimicking a parent, perhaps.)* 'They're both so devout and so determined to do Hajj in the middle of winter…/why should we stand in their way?'

ZAMURRUD: They'll condemn/ us.

HUSSAIN: They won't. We're betrothed.

ZAMURRUD: But they don't know / that.

HUSSAIN: Next time they see us we'll be husband and wife.

ZAMURRUD: I'll still have to live with the shame.

HUSSAIN: What shame? It was your idea to elope.

9

ZAMURRUD: Precisely.

HUSSAIN: Your idea to do Hajj in the middle of winter.

ZAMURRUD: I'm more religious than you.

HUSSAIN: I said, 'you must be crazy.' You said, 'you'd promise to marry me if I came with you.' I said, 'Done!' They'll forgive us. We're the same noble class, both Sunni, and we've been in love for as long as… Come here.

ZAMURRUD: No.

HUSSAIN: The first time I saw you, I thought the moon and stars shone in your eyes.

ZAMURRUD: We were six.

HUSSAIN: And ever since, my dearest Zamurrud, you've been rubies and coral to me! Amethysts and pearls. Come on! I'll warm / you up.

HUSSAIN makes a grab for her.

ZAMURRUD: Stop it.

HUSSAIN: You know I'll do anything for you.

ZAMURRUD: *(Trying to break free.)* Then let go. Hussain, stop it.

HUSSAIN lets her go.

I wish you were my brother.

HUSSAIN: We'll soon be related.

ZAMURRUD: If only I could stop thinking about him.

HUSSAIN: As soon as we get to Qazvin, I'll be your husband.

ZAMURRUD: *(Referring to her brother, Musa.)* I'm doing something we used to do together / and he'll be there.

HUSSAIN: Long before we get to Mecca.

ZAMURRUD: Not literally. The thought. Musa.

HUSSAIN: Family will understand. /They have to.

ZAMURRUD: Sometimes I hear the tone of his voice in the things I say.

HUSSAIN: They'll be happy for us.

ZAMURRUD: See his expression in my reflection. His gestures in the way I move… and I imagine what he might be thinking and doing… If only he were still alive.

HUSSAIN: Your family trusts me.

(Referring to the food he has unpacked.)

Are you hungry?

ZAMURRUD: Not to know for certain how he died… Or where he's buried…

HUSSAIN: *(About the food.)* There's time, / if you want to eat something.

ZAMURRUD: No place to grieve and pray for the safe journey of his soul. / Musa was a good man.

HUSSAIN: To Allah we belong and to Him we shall return.

ZAMURRUD: He knew this route like the back of his hand.

HUSSAIN: Wait till Judgement day, you'll see him again.

ZAMURRUD: What I don't understand is how Yakoob managed to survive?

HUSSAIN: When something happens as disastrous as losing your entire caravan of goods and your best friend, you'd think you could remember… Who? Where? Why?

ZAMURRUD: He says, 'Whoever it was, gave him something to drink, he went in to some sort of ecstatic state saw 'clouds' and fainted. And that's why they didn't kill him. / They thought he was dead.

HUSSAIN: Who though?

ZAMURRUD: He says, 'they saw a flock of fairies pouring out the caves likes bats.

HUSSAIN: This place is full of stories about fairies and giants. Most likely thieves, and Musa died defending himself. Although that doesn't explain how Yakoob –

ZAMURRUD: You think he killed him, don't you?

HUSSAIN: What's passed is past.

(Offering some food.)

Bread?

ZAMURRUD: It's easy for you to say.

HUSSAIN: It's a place we can't visit.

ZAMURRUD: Musa's grave?

HUSSAIN: The past.

ZAMURRUD: What if we could?.

HUSSAIN: We can't./ Life is today and tomorrow.

ZAMURRUD: Visit his grave?

HUSSAIN: We don't know where it is. Look at that sunset! The orange clouds –

ZAMURRUD: They're pink.

HUSSAIN: The orangey-pink clouds and the snowy peaks... They look like mangoes.

ZAMURRUD: No they don't.

HUSSAIN: Well, what do they look like?

ZAMURRUD: Snowy peaks.

HUSSAIN: Oh come on Zamurrud, cheer up. We're doing Hajj! And we're getting married!

(Offering her some picnic.)

Have some.

ZAMURRUD picks at some food.

Are you scared?

What are you scared of?

Snow leopards?

ZAMURRUD: They're more frightened of us than / we are of them.

HUSSAIN: Who says?

ZAMURRUD: Yakoob.

Enter two Batiniyah DISCIPLES.

DISCIPLE TWO: Where are you going?

HUSSAIN: Mecca. You?

DISCIPLE ONE: Alamut.

ZAMURRUD: *(Pointing.)* Is that that castle over there?

DISCIPLE TWO: No, that's Giri, and that's Samarin. The mountain crouching like a lion… See? That's Alamut … on its forehead… That's it.

DISCPLE ONE: Where are you from?

HUSSAIN: Aamil.

ZAMURRUD: What about you?

DISCIPLE TWO: Egypt.

ZAMURRUD: Batiniyah?

DISCIPLE TWO: Sunni?

DISCIPLE ONE: Wherever there is resistance to the truth we do the Khurshah's bidding.

ZAMURRUD: *(Passing him the letter.)* Then you must read / this.

HUSSAIN: Is it true that the first time the Khurshah, Imam Qayem Qayamat, saw Alamut, he tricked the owner into selling it to him, by offering him three thousand dinars for a bit of land nearby that was no bigger than the size of a buffalo skin? And then he cut the hide into thin, thin strips and tied them all together until they stretched right round the perimeter of the castle. And that's how he got it. For a bargain price. Is it true?

DISCIPLE TWO: Not Imam Qayem Qayamat, you fool, but the founder of the Batiniyah, Hassan-i-Sabbah.

ZAMURRUD: He knows that. Nearly two hundred years ago. It's the air up here / he goes all light-headed.

DISCIPLE ONE: He wasn't the real founder, though.

DISCIPLE TWO: He was.

DISCIPLE ONE: He wasn't.

HUSSAIN: He was.

ZAMURRUD: Actually maybe he wasn't.

DISCIPLE ONE: It was Nizar.

ZAMURRUD: Of course.

DISCIPLE TWO: Nizar?

DISCIPLE ONE: After the death of the seventh Imam, those who accepted the Fatimids, divided into two groups one supporting one son, Nizar and the other the other-… Al –Musta'lis. And then when Nizar died, Hassan Al Sabbah because of his loyalty to Nizar was expelled from Egypt and came to Persia.

DISCIPLE TWO: I know that, but –

HUSSAIN: So the Nizaris and the Batiniyah are the same?

DISCIPLE ONE: The same but not quite.

DISCIPLE TWO: And not beyond fighting each other on occasions.

HUSSAIN: It says in the Koran, 'that it is unlawful for a believer to kill another believer'.

DISCIPLE TWO: That all depends on what that person believes.

DISCIPLE ONE: If they don't believe what we believe.

HUSSAIN: We believe there is no true God but Allah, and Mohammed, peace be upon him, is the prophet of God. And if I'm honest with you, I'm ashamed that the history of our religion is defined by differences of opinion about the true meaning of the Prophet's words.

DISCIPLE ONE: May peace be upon him.

ZAMURRUD: As my father tells me it is with Christianity, and Juadism.

HUSSAIN: People choosing what they want to believe to suit their circumstances.

DISCIPLE TWO: Our faith is the one true faith, it makes our circumstances.

DISCIPLE ONE: We know the truth behind the truth, as revealed by our leader.

DISCIPLE TWO: And until there is unity of belief amongst all people we live to drive out the infidel, vanquish the oppressor, and be rewarded in Paradise.

HUSSAIN: Which oppressor?

ZAMURRUD: The Mongols, you fool.

DISCIPLE ONE: On all unbelievers is the curse of Allah.

HUSSAIN: But doesn't the Koran say, 'You cannot guide those you would like to but God guides those He wills. He has the best knowledge of the guided.'

ZAMURRUD: Let them read the letter Hussain

DISCIPLE ONE: It is not your job to interpret the word of God.

Pause.

DISCIPLE TWO reads the letter. To DISCIPLE ONE.

Read! From Abdul Rashied Bahr. They're under his instruction. He does our leader's biding in Aamil.

DISCIPLE ONE: They've a lot to learn.

DISCIPLE TWO: He says, 'their journey serves no other purpose than to do Hajj.

DISCIPLE ONE: If you want to stay alive, keep you're woozy Sunni thinking to yourself.

ZAMURRUD: He'll do his best.

DISCIPLE ONE: Dog!

DISCIPLE TWO: Come on, it's getting dark. As-salamu alaykum! Come on!

DISCIPLES leave.

ZAMURRUD: Why did we bother paying the chief apostate for the letter if you're not going to even pretend to be sympathetic to the Batiniyah – I don't understand you Hussain… /you'll get us both killed.

HUSSAIN: But how can they be so sure they have the one true faith?

ZAMURRUD: They're Batiniyah.

HUSSAIN picks up their bags.

I've got blisters.

HUSSAIN: Why didn't you say?

ZAMURRUD: I'm telling you now.

HUSSAIN: Let me dress them for you.

HUSSAIN tends to ZAMURRUD's feet.

Enter PASSERBY 1

PASSERBY 1: Quick, quick, quick, quick, QUICK!

Enter PASSERBY 2

PASSERSBY 2: That's the wrong way, I'm telling you!

PASSERBY 1 changing direction.

PASSERBY 1: Quick, quick, quick, quick QUICK!

PASSERSBY 2: This is my 'quick'!

PASSERSBY exit.

ZAMURRUD: Who's most likely to have killed Musa? Thieving pilgrims, rival merchants, the Batiniyah or the Mongols?

HUSSAIN: Yakoob? I don't know.

ZAMURRUD: Father says, 'ever since the Batiniyah assassinated Chughtai Khan, Gengis Khan's cousin, the Mongols have been threatening to invade Alamut, and perhaps they could've mistook –

HUSSAIN: They're not in Persia. Not yet.

ZAMURRUD: He says, they could be operating under cover, because Chughtai Khan's children have all sworn to avenge their father's killing. Even Princess Balghan Khatoon, who rumour has it can snatch a captive as easily as a hawk a chicken.' Their women are as formidable as the men.'

HUSSAIN: But no match for the Batiniyah, surely? I don't see any blisters.

ZAMURRUD: They claim the same divine mandate to rule the world. On the heel... At the bottom.

HUSSAIN: But my Uncle says, if you don't challenge Mongol supremacy, and offer them hospitality and the opportunity to share your faith, he says –

ZAMURRUD: *(About her heel.)* Oiw! / That's so sore!

HUSSAIN: They'll leave you alone.

ZAMURRUD: Unlike the Batiniyah.

HUSSAIN: Who claim the soul of Islam for themselves.

ZAMURRUD: You don't have to keep telling me.

HUSSAIN: Which would you rather be ruled by, Mongols or Batiniyah?

ZAMURRUD: Neither.

HUSSAIN: But if you had a choice.

ZAMURRUD: It won't happen.

HUSSAIN: But if it did? There!

ZAMURRUD: There's one on the ball of my foot.

HUSSAIN: In the Koran it says, 'we were created from a single pairing of a male and female, and then made into nations and tribes - that we may know each other, not that we may despise each other'.

ZAMURRUD: All our religious disputes only stem from differences of opinion about the truth of the Prophet's succession. Peace be upon him.

HUSSAIN: But how can anyone know the truth unless they were there to witness it?

PASSERSBY 3 & 4 enter.

PASSERBY THREE: It's the right way I'm telling you.

PASSERBY FOUR: It's not. Good evening.

ZAMURRUD: Hello.

PASSERBY THREE: It is.

HUSSAIN: Where are you trying to get to?

PASSERBY THREE: I've read the map. We don't need to ask. It's the right way. I've a better sense of direction than you.

PASSERBY FOUR: You don't. Good bye.

PASSERSBY leave.

HUSSAIN: And when all the witnesses are dead, all we have is their accounts of the truth passed on… interpreted in many different ways.

ZAMURRUD: What are you talking about?

HUSSAIN: The truth. The truth about whether Mohammed, peace be upon him, nominated a successor or not.

ZAMURRUD: The truth is what the majority choose it to be.

HUSSAIN: Or what they are <u>made</u> to choose. My Uncle says we are two people at the same time. And it is important to know the truth about who we are as individuals and the truth about the group we represent.

ZAMURRUD: Your point?

HUSSAIN: I believe, everyone is born with a conscience just as they are born with common sense. It is what separates us from the beasts. When we do something wrong we feel guilty. When do something good it gives us pleasure.

ZAMURRUD: But we still need religion.

HUSSAIN: Do we? Why? When our conscience can guide us instinctively?

ZAMURRUD: To guide and protect our morality. / I'm religious.

HUSSAIN: So am I. But sometimes don't you wonder why?

ZAMURRUD: What are you saying? How can I marry you if you are not religious?

HUSSAIN: It seems to me that the minute someone tells me what I should be thinking and I choose to believe them, I'm probably lying to myself. Come on!

ZAMURRUD: What, even when it is our Imam? Your Uncle? What are you talking about? Have you gone mad?

HUSSAIN sets off.

That's the wrong way.

HUSSAIN: No it's not.

ZAMURRUD: We should follow the canal.

HUSSAIN: We'll never make it.

ZAMURRUD: It's quicker.

HUSSAIN: It isn't. You can't get through the forest in the valley. / It's so thick, the sunlight never touches the floor.

ZAMURRUD: It's quicker than over the top… and the sooner we're married the better.

HUSSAIN: It isn't. I know the best way.

ZAMURRUD: I do.

Three more RECRUITS pass.

RECRUIT THREE: As-salamu aleikum. Wrong way.

HUSSAIN: Waleiykum assalam. If you're looking for Alamut, it's that way.

RECRUIT THREE: Jazak Allah Khair.

HUSSAIN: Fi Ammanullah.

RECRUITS leave.

Everyone says –

ZAMURRUD: Who's everyone?

HUSSAIN: You know, the forest down there is full of man-eating giants and blood-sucking fairies.

ZAMURRUD: You can't scare me.

HUSSAIN: Like a mist of wasps, with little bead heads… and the shrunken faces of their victims.

ZAMURRUD: You don't believe that.

HUSSAIN: Flying to sting the unsuspecting traveller with human-teeth-tipped arrows dripping poison. Ask Yakoob, if you don't believe me?

ZAMURRUD: Yakoob says there's this amazing clearing in that forest. A meadow of wild flowers – by the Virinjan canal where it's warm even in winter… /The best place to get a good night's sleep.

HUSSAIN: They'll leave you twitching and gasping for breath as they ingest you, body and soul.

ZAMURRUD: And in the left corner looking away from the water – that's where I'll find Musa's grave.

HUSSAIN: What?

ZAMURRUD: That's where he's buried.

HUSSAIN: What did you say?

ZAMURRUD: To be honest I didn't see any point in telling you the real reason why I wanted to do Hajj with you.

HUSSAIN: Sorry?

ZAMURRUD: It isn't because I'm devoutly religious, although I am. It isn't because I want to marry you, although I do, / but not immediately –

HUSSAIN: What?

ZAMURRUD: It's because Yakoob told me that Musa died in the valley down there by the Virinjan canal, and you must allow me to grieve at his grave.

HUSSAIN: But –

ZAMURRUD: And if I'm going to die there I'd rather die in your arms.

HUSSAIN: So you've tricked /me –

ZAMURRUD: And the fairies Musa and Yakoob saw were nothing like your wasps. He told my parents – I wasn't supposed to be listening, but they left the door open and I was sitting on the stairs – 'the fairies were beautiful women… the most beautiful women he'd ever seen… who bewitched him and Musa with their singing and their dancing… and oiling their hair and bathing in the warm water of the canal.' Yakoob says, 'he and Musa, thought they were dreaming until they realized they were both dreaming the same dream therefore it had to be for real. They believed they'd stumbled on paradise.' The meadow was like a garden, and the things they were offered, especially this special wine, infused with hashish which they were told was halal.

HUSSAIN: What's hashish?

21

ZAMURRUD: The wine. He said he'd never tasted anything like it, or experienced the tricks it played with his imagination. Two cups and he felt so relaxed he thought he was a cloud.

HUSSAIN: He thought he was a cloud? / I thought he just saw clouds?

ZAMURRUD: That's what he said. And they were told, 'they'd only have to pray twice a day and there was no need for ablutions after conjugation.'

HUSSAIN: What?

ZAMURRUD: He was talking to my parents.

HUSSAIN: They had sex in a field with loads of beautiful women?

ZAMURRUD: He didn't say exactly, but he said, 'he had these amazing happy thoughts and started smiling like a new moon and jabbering lovely words. Poetry to the angels.' Yakoob says, 'the last he saw of Musa... he'd never seen him so happy... he saw him strip off and grab one of the angels – he preferred to call them angels than fairies – '

HUSSAIN: But they were real women, you're saying?

ZAMURRUD: He said, 'that's what they felt like.' And as he tore at her clothes... she screamed but it came out as a song... a beautiful love song and then he saw colours rippling in his eyes, and his knees started to wobble and he went cold and fainted.

HUSSAIN: Musa?

ZAMURRUD: Yakoob. And when he woke up he found my brother lying dead beside him and the place was deserted.

HUSSAIN: And you believe him?

ZAMURRUD: He dug a grave with his bare hands and carved Musa's name in the rock. And there he kept vigil for days, months... hoping whoever had poured out of the mountain that night to play in the field, would return and kill him.

But they didn't. And eventually, convinced that whoever had killed Musa wouldn't kill him... because he wasn't worthy... and overcome with shame for having been under the influence of the wine... he decided to seek penitence... to spend the rest of his life a hermit... but not until he'd come back to Aamil and told my parents what he knew.

HUSSAIN: And is this the real reason why / you –

ZAMURRUD: Yes. It's the truth. I know it is, because the day after Yakoob said what he said, I dreamt of Musa. And in the dream Musa charged me to visit his grave in the meadow and pray for the safe journey of his soul to paradise. He wouldn't have told me if Yakoob –

HUSSAIN: You believe a dream? You've lied to me.

ZAMURRUD: If I don't tell you something it doesn't make it a lie.

HUSSAIN: How can we be together if you're going to lie to me?

ZAMURRUD: I love you.

HUSSAIN: You've betrayed me.

ZAMURRUD: *(Going to touch him.)* I haven't betrayed you.

HUSSAIN: Don't touch me.

ZAMURRUD: You said you'd do anything for me.

HUSSAIN: But why didn't you tell me?

ZAMURRUD: Because you wouldn't have come with me.

Pause.

You don't have to come.

HUSSAIN: I'm not letting you go on your own.

ZAMURRUD: If I die –

HUSSAIN: You're not going to die.

ZAMURRUD: Promise me you'll tell my parents where, when and how –

HUSSAIN: You've promised your life to me.

ZAMURRUD: And ask them to forgive me.

HUSSAIN: For what?

ZAMURRUD: Please, wipe the dishonour from my name. Tell them I died chaste.

Pause

HUSSAIN: Tomorrow. Let's go tomorrow. Tonight we'll spend / up here –

ZAMURRUD: You're not scared are you?

HUSSAIN: We'll have a look for the field on the way back…/ In the morning.

ZAMURRUD: If you love me, as much as you say you love me, you'll come with me to pray for Musa's soul.

Are you coming?

Pause.

Good bye, then.

ZAMURRUD walks off on her own.

HUSSAIN hesitates and then rushes to catch up with her. Music.

SCENE TWO

In a meadow by the Virinjan Canal. HUSSAIN loses ZAMURRUD.

Silence. Complete darkness. A horn sounds. Strange eerie noises. Singing in the distance getting louder. Strange light, enhanced with a firefly dance of torch light.

HUSSAIN: Blood sucking fairies!

ZAMURRUD: Angels.

HUSSAIN & ZAMURRUD: Beautiful women.

HOURIS, all uniformly dressed, holding torches, pour into a beautiful moonlit meadow, dancing and singing as though released from a tedious lesson to play.

HOURIS: *(Sing – and the song continues under the dialogue.)*

Last night we dreamt of Paradise
Four rivers in gardens of light,
One for the spirit, the essence, the heart
One to rescue the soul.

We flocked as angels on the summer's breeze.
To the land of fruit and flowers
Beside rivers of milk, honey and gold,
We settled in harmony.

Here God would save us from our selves,
From promises left unfulfilled
To friends we made but then betrayed
With lies and gross misdeeds.

God extends forgiveness
With acts of kindness and love
As he gathers our souls like pearls of wheat
to sow in heaven above.

Last night we dreamt of Paradise
Four rivers in gardens of light,
One for the spirit, the essence, the heart
One to rescue the soul.

MUSTAFA's horn sounds again and they disperse to perform their ablutions and in doing so reveal HUSSAIN, and ZAMURRUD in tears, praying for forgiveness at MUSA's roughly-made and crudely marked grave. After a while MARJAN, a young houri, breaks ranks and rushes to the grave.

MARJAN: *(To ZAMURRUD.)* Go away! Get out! /Go on! / Before they capture you.

HUSSAIN: Leave her alone!

MARJAN: And take me with you!

PARISA, an older houri, approaches.

PARISA: Marjan!

25

(To HUSSAIN and ZAMURRUD.)

This is our field.

MARJAN: I told them to go.

HUSSAIN: We've come to pray –

PARISA: *(To HUSSAIN and ZAMURRUD.)* Look how pretty! As pretty as a morning rose. Look at her ankles.

HUSSAIN: We've come to pray for the safe passage of her brother's soul.

PARISA: Was he a good man? Pretty …Marjan, so pretty, very, pretty…

ZAMURRUD: Yes, of course he was.

PARISA: Then why pray for him? Pretty. Gazelle.

HUSSAIN: Who knows what he might have done that could separate him from the life to come? / Better be safe than sorry.

ZAMURRUD: We don't know how he died.

MARJAN: The same way they all do around here.

PARISA: Wait till the Khurshah sets eyes on her.

ZAMURRUD: How did he die?

MUSTAFA approaches with a stone vase of wine.

MUSTAFA: *(Approaching with the wine.)* 'Let the believer of Allah and the day of judgement honour his guest'. Have some wine, my friends.

ZAMURRUD: *(Refusing the wine.)* It's not permitted.

PARISA: *(About the wine.)* Our Imam says we can.

HUSSAIN: That's a shame because ours says, 'we can't.'

ZAMURRUD: *(Thrusting the letter at PARISA.)* I have a letter here from the chief apostate in Aamil.

MARJAN: Sunni.

PARISA: Obviously. The whiff of privilege is everywhere about them. And she is ravishing. She is a delight. My pretty, pretty gazelle.

HUSSAIN: We don't believe in the superiority of our faith. As long as people believe in something it doesn't matter to us what you believe in.

ZAMURRUD: Of course it does. He's only saying that because of the altitude… the thin air… it affects his brain.

HUSSAIN: We're in the valley.

ZAMURRUD: What he means is as long as those who believe fight in the cause of Allah.

HUSSAIN: 'There is no compulsion where religion is concerned.'

ZAMURRUD: Shut up Hussain.

PARISA: What's your name?

HUSSAIN: Hussain.

PARISA: Obviously. Her name? Your name my pretty, pretty gazelle?

HUSSAIN: I'm Hussain and this is my betrothed, Zamurrud.

ZAMURRUD: We're doing Hajj.

HUSSAIN: And getting married on the way /… in Qazvin.

PARISA: You're very pretty. Gazelle.

ZAMURRUD: I am flattered that you think I'm beautiful but please stop calling me a gazelle. I can't help feeling I'll be devoured by a lion.

MARJAN: *(About HUSSAIN.)* Handsome.

MUSTAFA: *(Offering the wine.)* Here, very, very nice wine! Brewed from the dazzling dates and gorgeous grapes grown in this valley.

HUSSAIN takes a glass.

ZAMURRUD: No Hussain.

PARISA: Masha Allah.

MUSTAFA: Masha Allah. Infused with local herbs to enhance your performance and guarantee sweet dreams.

ZAMURRUD: We can't. It is forbidden /us.

MARJAN: Drink some. It would be rude not to accept our hospitality.

HUSSAIN: That's very kind of you. But really it is against our faith.

PARISA: If you want to stay safe…

MARJAN: Mustafa must be obeyed. He's the Khurshah's head eunuch.

PARISA: He's sings like the nightingale. You like to sing for us don't you Mustafa?

MUSTAFA: Oh yes, yes. Singing is my desire.

PARISA: This valley is famous for its nightingales. Can you hear them?

They listen to the sound of nightingales and MUSTAFA starts to sing.

MUSTAFA: *(Sing – song continues under dialogue.)*
I'm so grateful to you Allah
For the life you've given me
And the Prophet's words to overcome
My deep uncertainties

HUSSAIN: We can't stay long.

MUSTAFA: Brave Allah I'll stand firm and strong
To defeat your enemies
For you've shone a light
On my frail heart
And set my poor soul free.
/ Allah! Allah! Allah!
Allah!

ZAMURRUD: Promise me Hussain if I die here, you'll bury me under these stones?

HUSSAIN: Whoever buries you will have to bury me too.

(To PARISA.)

Thank you for your kind offer of hospitality but as soon as she has prayed for her brother's soul we must be going.

PARISA: *(To MARJAN.)* But it is the lovely evening. Summer in the shadow of winter is the best summer ever. Ask the young man to dance?

MARJAN: *(To HUSSAIN.)* Dance?

PARISA: Imagine his expressive belly and the contours of his muscles. Do you like dancing, Hussain? If you are looking to free the soul. They say dancing does the trick.

ZAMURRUD: Really, do none of you know what happened to my brother?

MUSTAFA: /He died.

MARJAN: I'll tell you, if you dance with me.

PARISA: We have no idea how that grave came to be in our field but I know someone who does.

MARJAN: Please dance with me?

PARISA: The Khurshah's mother.

ZAMURRUD: I'd be grateful for any news.

MARJAN: Take her inside and we'll wait here for you.

HUSSAIN: No, I want to hear what she has to say.

PARISA: I'm afraid our mother isn't very well and will only meet people one at a time. Her skin is as yellow as a bad lemon. It's best if – sorry what did you say your name was?

MUSTAFA: Zamurrud.

PARISA: Zamurrud comes alone. You stay young man. Marjan will look after you. Mustafa watch she behaves and doesn't leave the field with him.

HUSSAIN: *(Handing her the apostate's letter.)* Take the letter. Just in case.

ZAMURRUD: Don't drink that wine.

HUSSAIN: Of course not.

MUSTAFA: But the Khurshah says, 'the Koran makes it perfectly clear it was permissible before it was forbidden.'

PARISA: If you'll not let him accept our hospitality how can I take you to see the Khurshah's mother?

MUSTAFA: Drink.

PARISA: She'll never learn the fate of her brother if you don't.

HUSSAIN: Go on, Zamurrud it's what you came for. I'll be all right.

PARISA: Come on.

HUSSAIN: Yakoob survived, didn't he?

HUSSAIN drinks.

PARISA: There. Not so bad, eh?

(To ZAMURRUD.)

Come on, my little gazelle. / Come meet the lion.

ZAMURRUD: I'm not your gazelle.

PARISA and ZAMURRUD leave. MUSTAFA standing in attendance with a jug of wine and a tray containing two glasses.

MUSTAFA: Very good. Very good. Some more wine Hussain?

HUSSAIN: *(Takes a glass and drinks.)* It's delicious.

MARJAN: Where are you from?

HUSSAIN: You?

MUSTAFA and the HOURIS start to sing.

30

MUSTAFA: *(Offering him some wine.)* Egypt.

HUSSAIN: Really?

MARJAN: I'm from Yemen.

HUSSAIN: This wine's delicious. / Yemen? How did you get here?

MUSTAFA: Renowned for releasing the memory from the sadness of living, enhancing perception, relaxing the body and increasing performance.

HUSSAIN: You said.

MARJAN: It's a long story. Have some more and I'll tell it to you.

HUSSAIN downs another glass.

HUSSAIN: Wow!

MARJAN: Go on. Have another.

HUSSAIN: Well here come the clouds!

MUSTAFA: *(To MARJAN.)* Now pleasure him!

HUSSAIN: *(Feeling the effects of the brew.)* Here come Yakoob's clouds! Huge magenta clouds float by in a turquoise sky, and I wonder why it is… and why are we…

MARJAN: Then leave us alone, you pickled fool.

HUSSAIN: Bleeding purple rain, draining through a keyhole of light…

MARJAN: If you want to watch stand back.

HUSSAIN: Turning the bone in the lock

MUSTAFA: *(Threatening MARJAN with a stick.)* Go on.

HUSSAIN: In the room with no walls that are running away.

MARJAN: You go on.

MUSTAFA: If you want me to tell Parisa –

HUSSAIN: Flying bread raining mustard seed.

MARJAN: Only if you promise you'll release me.

MUSTAFA: *(Lifting his stick.)* Do it or you won't be allowed in the field for a week. Go on!

MARJAN cowers.

HUSSAIN: A host of marching tongues, bobbing up and down like bubbles in the lake… lick, lick, licking…

MARJAN approaches HUSSAIN uncommitted to the idea of pleasuring him.

MARJAN: Do you like my ankles?

HUSSAIN: *(Taking another drink.)* Well… yes… they look lovely… like… ankles.

MUSTAFA: Show them! You're not showing them!

MARJAN: *(Showing her ankles.)* What? What do they look like?

HUSSAIN: Lotus bulbs.

MUSTAFA: *(Laughs.)*

MARJAN: No they don't.

MUSTAFA: And her thighs are like water melons in the season of water melons.

HUSSAIN: Figs.

MARJAN: Figs?

HUSSAIN: In the season of figs.

MUSTAFA: Figs?

MARJAN: My thighs?

HUSSAIN: Show me your paws.

MARJAN: I'm not a rabbit.

HUSSAIN: The apricot under your sail.

MARJAN: The hashish has taken your mind

MUSTAFA: What about her breasts?

HUSSAIN: Pomegranates.

MUSTAFA: *(Threatening to beat her.)* Show him!

MARJAN: Do you want to see my breasts Hussain?

HUSSAIN: Well…

MARJAN: Do you want to see them?

Pause.

HUSSAIN: Swarms of locusts are flying through my brain, stripping my desire and I'm limping home.

MARJAN: He doesn't want to see me!

HUSSAIN: I am betrothed to the most beautiful Eve in the world. The sky is grey and white and falling. I love Zamurrud! And cloudy magenta. Orangey-mango. But when the truth shines through her I love her more than love itself! I'll love her until I die and in the life after I'll love her until it stops raining…!

MUSTAFA: *(Threatening MARJAN again.)* Show him! Show him!

MARJAN: *(Grabbing hold of HUSSAIN for protection.)* Please kiss me. Hold me tight. Stroke my cheek and tell me –

MUSTAFA: But I can't!

MARJAN: *(Whispers.)* Rescue me!

MUSTAFA: *(Pulling MARJAN off HUSSAIN.)* Speak up!

HUSSAIN attacks MUSTAFA but is knocked out by him. ZAMURRUD rushes back with the Houris and Batiniyah Disciples.

ZAMURRUD: Quick, Hussain. Quick, we must leave immediately –

PARISA: Catch her! Don't let her escape! For the Khurshah!

They trap ZAMURRUD. They gag her and bundle her away. MARJAN lingers with HUSSAIN's body. MUSTAFA threatens to beat MARJAN if she doesn't leave immediately. She leaves. MUSTAFA adds ZAMURRUD's name to the grave.

SCENE THREE

Waking to find ZAMURRUD has disappeared HUSSAIN looks for her everywhere, before discovering that she is in her brother's grave.

HUSSAIN: *(Calling till his voice breaks.)* ZAMURRRRUDDDD!

She is dead. I am alive. My unhappiness is to survive. If it wasn't against my religion I'd impale myself on that tree, I'd dig myself into this grave … Lie here with you until we rub bones. In death grinding each other to dust. If only my faith would let me take my own life, I'd cleave my head and sod the earth with my brains.

I'm not doing Hajj anymore, I'm not going back to Aamil… For the rest of my wretched life I'm staying here.

Parisa, Marjan! Mustafa! Come out from where ever you're hiding! Kill me, why don't you?! Wherever you lurk in the misery of these mountains show yourselves.

Please my dearest Zamurrud… Zamurrud call for me in a dream, as you said Musa called to you.

Thoughts of you will be my qiblah, your grave my mosque.

SCENE FOUR

Living off leaves, grasses and the odd bird he could snare HUSSAIN spent six months mourning the death of his beloved. Then one morning whilst he was out searching for food, two Houris return with a letter from ZAMURRUD.

The meadow. PARISA massages MARJAN's scalp with fragrant oils. MUSTAFA at a distance, seemingly asleep.

PARISA: Now where's he gone?

MARJAN: He won't have gone far.

Anyway, as I was saying I lived in the house of old Ali.

PARISA: The Khurshah's impatient to get this sorted… As we all are.

MARJAN: And Old Ali and his son Young Ali, were both very successful merchants, / hundreds of camels, silk and spices –

PARISA: As we all are. Until Hussain leaves this field it's out of bounds for us.

MARJAN: They're happy to assassinate their enemies, why don't they do the same to him?

PARISA: Because the Khurshah doesn't want to make a martyr of him. He wants Zamurrud to love him, of her own free will. You've seen what he's like, moping about the castle, as depressed as the setting sun…

MARJAN: He's besotted with her. He's worse with her than he was with any of us.

PARISA: Not with me.

MARJAN: Of course not Parisa, everyone knows you were the finest lover between Kabul and Samarkand.

PARISA: Laugh if you don't believe me but it's true. The Khurshah needs her to give up her love for Hussain. And he doesn't believe she will, unless we can persuade her that Hussain has given up his love for her.

MARJAN: I'm sure when he reads our letter.

PARISA: You say that, but the Khurshah's not convinced.

MARJAN: That's because he wants it too much. / And is so impatient.

PARISA: He says the only way is to persuade Hussain to convert to Batiniyah. Then in true obedience to his leader, our Khurshah, he will have no option but to renounce his love for Zamurrud, when he is called to do so.

MARJAN: Which will be immediately! With so many to choose from why does he have to pick the one who is betrothed?

PARISA: In my experience men are always more attracted by what they can't have than what is being offered to them on a plate. Where's he got to?/ Have you got her letter there?

MARJAN: Don't worry. He'll be back. Anyway as I was saying... the young Ali was killed by robbers. And because the older old Ali –

PARISA: Old Ali?

MARJAN: Older Ali relied on his son the Younger Ali, to keep his four wives and seven children. Well, you can imagine... it wasn't long before the family were in debt and his wives told him to sell me, as my mother and I had been sold to him, by my relatives.

PARISA: I was abducted by the Turks... became the chieftain's wife until – it's the same story – I was sold to his creditor, who sold me on to his creditor, who sold me to his creditor, and so on and so forth until I was rescued by a Batiniyah disciple.

MARJAN: Rescued? You're still someone's property. I am all in all a human being who belongs to myself and no one else. We all are.

Old Ali's wives were much kinder to me than they had been to my mother. They bullied her and threw her in the well. I was taken to the market in Bukarah and bought for the gardens, by Mustafa who swore by the beard of the prophet I would live here like a Princess.

PARISA: Were you your master's wife by then?

MARJAN: What do you mean?

Enter HUSSAIN.

PARISA: Quick, hide! He mustn't see us!

MARJAN: You mean was I still a virgin? Do you think, Parisa if I hadn't lost my virginity I'd be the Khurshah's queen and he'd be treating me as he treats Zamurrud?

PARISA: Well...

MARJAN: Thanks to your powders the Khurshah had no idea I wasn't a virgin.

PARISA: I don't know. He seems to love her with a love I've never seen him show before.

MARJAN: No one has ever loved me.

Enter HUSSAIN. The HOURIS dash for cover. HUSSAIN unfolds ZAMURRUD's clothes, lays them out on the gravestone, meticulously. He does this repeatedly throughout the scene.

PARISA: You stupid man. Can't you understand. She's not coming back. The next time you meet will be on the day of judgement.

MARJAN: He's not stupid he's in love.

PARISA: We'll have to be careful – wait.

Beat.

MARJAN: Parisa, is it true that the Christians and the Jews eat their own children?

(In a whisper.)

Is it?

PARISA: Who told you that?

MARJAN: Mustafa.

PARISA: They do what they do at the command of whoever they believe in.

MARJAN: As we do at the command of the Khurshah.

Pause.

PARISA: The command of Allah as interpreted by the Khurshah, Imam Qayem Qayamat, The Light of Lights. The first after Allah, and Imam to all Batiniyah.

MARJAN: I know, I know he's very clever, and says the rewards promised us on the Day of Judgement will be infinitely more than those promised by other religions, but why can't we keep our babies?

PARISA: We must suffer so that God may see who is truly righteous. The agonies and struggles of our lives have a purpose for God. God uses suffering to look within us, and correct the unbelievers. Through suffering our souls are cleansed.

Beat.

(To HUSSAIN who can't hear her.)

You stupid man, stop grieving and leave!

MARJAN: But why should the babies suffer? They didn't ask to be born. I am haunted by their writhing bodies and their cries as the vultures pick the flesh off their bones.

PARISA: He should stop doing that ridiculous thing with her clothes.

MARJAN: I can't understand their love for each other.

PARISA: That's because no one's ever vowed to marry you.

MARJAN: If he knew the gifts the Khurshah was giving her he'd know how pointless it was expecting her to come for her clothes when she's got the best wardrobe in Paradise.

HUSSAIN: *(Audibly praying.)*

PARISA: Where's our letter?

MARJAN: He'll never stop loving her.

PARISA: Come on, let's give him the letter. I'll distract him while you drop it on the grave.

MARJAN: Do you think he'll recognise the handwriting.

PARISA: Of course he will. She wrote it.

MARJAN: At our command.

PARISA: It's the words I worry about. She's so posh.

PARISA starts to hum a song. The sound is inconsistent and very quiet just enough to distracts HUSSAIN. He walks away from the grave while MARJAN places the letter on the gravestone, unseen.

HUSSAIN: Hello? Who is it? Is there anybody there? Is that you Zamurrud? There's nobody there. I'm so hungry I'm hallucinating.

HUSSAIN returns, finds the letter on the grave.

(Seeing it and tentatively picking up the folded paper.)

How can this – ? From Zamurrud?

(Reading the letter.)

'Hussain, I am happy in the Garden of Eden, that is promised to every Muslim and God-fearing person in the Koran'.

(Shrieks with delight.)

Joy, above unrelenting joy! My love is in paradise!

'The place is beyond your wildest dreams. / Pleasures unimaginable…

MARJAN: *(Reading from a rough copy of the same letter or unseen over his shoulder.)* '…pleasures unimaginable as promised to every Muslim and God fearing person in the Koran.' But despite all the spiritual delights on offer, nothing compares to the memory of you. It is like a thorn in my soul. I am missing you… missing you /most terribly. I am missing you'.

HUSSAIN: *(Rereading.)* 'Most terribly… I am missing you…' Me too.

'The angels and other spirits' –

MARJAN & PARISA: That's us.

HUSSAIN: *(Reading.)* '… Tell me you keep constant vigil at my grave and I have sneaked back to see you but I couldn't reveal myself or cry out. I so want to see your face, to hear you, and caress you. I am hurting with desire.

PARISA: That's good.

HUSSAIN: *(Reading.)* 'So much… I've been told that it's because it is still linked – my desire – to the world of matter, and that soon my soul will expunge it'. Expunge it?

PARISA: Expunge!

HUSSAIN: *(Reading.)* That doesn't sound very Zamurrud. Expunge? 'I'm sorry that I can't reveal myself to you. I have wept at your weeping. And I'm weeping now in the sound of the rustling polar leaves –

PARISA: That's very Zamurrud.

MARJAN: That was my idea.

PARISA: – in the knowledge that our union is a distant happiness. We must suffer apart, until the time comes, when we will be two souls united. Until such time, dearest Hussain, please ease my suffering by carrying out my last wish'.

PARISA & MARJAN & HUSSAIN: 'Please… please, please just go away… and forget about me'

HUSSAIN: 'I have been home to Aamil. Like you they could not see me. They have not forgiven us for eloping. They slander and defame me.' Defame?

MARJAN: I told you he wouldn't understand it.

PARISA: He doesn't believe it…

HUSSAIN: 'Since you can't relieve me of the pain of not being able to be with you, please relieve me of their calumny' – Calumny? What does that mean? – / and go home'

PARISA: Character assassination, you fool.

HUSSAIN: 'Please relieve me of my shame and go to Aamil and tell them what has happened.'

MARJAN: 'Your far-removed / and adoring, Zamurrud.'

HUSSAIN: '… removed and adoring Zamurrud.'

(Calling to the air.)

Zamurrud, oh Zamurrud you know I'd be lying in this grave if I could contact angels you command… Wherever they are? Wherever you are, listen! Please listen to me!

MARJAN: I wish we could all be as convinced of the after life as Hussain.

PARISA: We houris know better than most, how susceptible the mind is to believe what it wants.

HUSSAIN: I can't go back to Aamil, Zamurrud. You know, no one's going to believe, or forgive me. Try as hard as I might to remind them of your piety, your innocence and your spirituality without you being there… no. Please, I don't want you to take advantage of your position in Paradise, but couldn't you use your influence to call for me, and ask Allah, God be merciful, to end my life sooner rather than later… rather then send me on a humiliating, pointless mission to ask for understanding and forgiveness which they're never going to grant? My pain is your pain, and they will banish me, or worse get me to admit to an untruth. And if I lie what chance have I got of ever being with you on Judgement day? Tell whoever it is that has killed you and Musa to kill me, too.

PARISA: The Khurshah was right.

MARJAN: So, what are we going to do?

PARISA: Get him to convert to Batiniyah.

(Producing another letter.)

Letter two. I made her write it by threatening to have Mustafa assassinate Hussain.

Give it to him.

Through misdirection PARISA throws another letter on the stone without HUSSAIN seeing how it got there. MARJAN and PARISA start to sing in an eerie heavenly chorus SONG 3 (reprise SONG 1) as HUSSAIN eyes the letter suspiciously.

HUSSAIN: *(Opening the letter.)* 'Beloved Hussain, I have consulted the Light of Lights… Prepare to meet me.

(Yelping with joy.)

Whoa! That was quick!

You heard me!

PARISA: *(Reading over his shoulder.)* 'I'm nearby but far away'.

HUSSAIN: What's that supposed to mean? Zamurrud! Where are you? Zamurrud!

(Reading.)

'You must leave this meadow and go to the western valleys of mount Ararat straight away.'

/What are you doing there?

MARJAN: How's Zamurrud going to get to mount Ararat?

PARISA: She's not. That's where Hussain's going to find a new spiritual leader and guide, part of the Batiniyah inner circle, Shareef Ali Vujoodi –

HUSSAIN: *(Reading.)* 'There's a cave on the western side of the mountain where many divinely enlightened young recruits complete forty days mystic seclusion as part of their preparations to visit paradise.'

MARJAN: Is that where they're only allowed to eat every fourth day?

PARISA: And even then only a bowl of vegetables.

HUSSAIN: Great, it says here, I get to die.

PARISA: No you won't –

HUSSAIN: *(Reading on.)* Oh…

PARISA: Not yet. When you're in a fit state to meditate –

HUSSAIN: *(Reading.)* 'Meditate on me.' …On you Zamurrud? For forty days? Easy. You're always on my mind… Let's go. I'm ready. 'One face, Zamurrud's, one thought, to meet Shareef Ali Vujoodi'.

MARJAN: I thought to become a true disciple you had to do a lot more than that?

PARISA: Then he's got to go to the most famous crypt in Shahr-e-Khaleel and meditate for another forty days between the graves of the prophets Jacob and Joseph. To lie between their mummified effigies without dying of fear or being discovered, and pray. Pray, pray, pray!

HUSSAIN: 'And though you may frequently see me beckoning to you to leave before your time is up, don't let the hallucinations of the imagination deceive you. People will try and stop you –

MARJAN: Still only eating every fourth day?

PARISA: Absolutely. Only vegetables. The more you suffer the greater the reward, remember.

HUSSAIN: *(Reading.)* 'Then with your mind and body cleansed and focussed, head for Aleppo, and in the Ramna district – how am I supposed to remember all this? I'd better not lose this letter – where you will find a small mosque known as Samaneen… known as Samaneen. At dawn prayers you will see amongst the congregation a wise man, wearing rough woollen clothes and a green turban. A green turban, because he is a Fatimid Syed and descendant of the holy prophet, peace be upon him.'

MARJAN: But not Imam Qayem Qayamet.

HUSSAIN: 'Shaikh Shareef Ali Vujoodi, known as Valley of Sinai, by initiates of the 'World of Light'. Batiniyah.

PARISA: Shareef Ali Vujoodi knows the Khurshah well.

HUSSAIN: *(Continuing to read.)* He will appear humble in temperament and dress, but his eyes will blaze with intense spirituality. If you love and desire me you will serve and obey him until your purpose is served.

(Reads the line again.)

If you love and desire me you will serve and obey him until your purpose is served'.

My purpose being to see you in Paradise, Zamurrud.

'If, after a year,' A year?

PARISA: 'I know it might seem like a long time, but if you are committed to your task it will pass in no time at all, and we will be reunited. If you do everything Shaikh Shareef Ali Vujoodi asks of, without resentment and to the best of your abilities, with utter devotion, then he'll choose his moment to tell you that he has the power to send you to paradise and meet me.'

HUSSAIN: 'And at that point you prostrate yourself at his feet and let him know how much a visit would mean to you and he'll arrange it. Believe me. Until we meet again. Your faithful Zamurrud'.

Alhamdulillah!

MARAJAN: If Zamurrud hasn't succumbed to the Khurshah's advances by the time Hussain has done all that I'll eat her clothes.

HUSSAIN folds up the letter and ZAMURRUD's clothes and prepares to leave.

MARJAN: Has he got enough food for the journey?

PARISA: Plenty and much nicer than what he's been living on.

HUSSAIN discovers a bag full of provisions.

HUSSAIN: Thanks be to Allah!

PARISA: And as soon as he's out of the valley. He'll find a fresh donkey waiting for him.

MARJAN: You've thought of everything.

HUSSAIN leaves.

PARISA: The field is ours again!

SCENE FIVE

As Zamurrud had instructed, Hussain spent forty nights
In a cave on the slopes of Mount Ararat
The place where Prophet Abraham's believed to have seen
The Creator in the rising and the setting of the stars.

He reluctantly survived on a diet of vegetables
Eating every fourth day, to free his mind
To meditate on Zamurrud's enchanting face
And the written instructions she had left behind.

Cave task completed he then had to reach
The holy city of Shaahr-e-Khalil
To creep into the mosque there without being caught
And spend a night alone with the bodies in the crypt.

Between Joseph and Jacob the mummified prophets
It took a mammoth leap of faith not to be scared
To summon Zamurrud's face as he'd done in the cave
And imagine how soon he'd be in Paradise with her

Spending as long in the crypt as he had in the cave
Hussain emerged triumphant but nearly got killed
By the locals who were seeking a bloodthirsty revenge
For the Batiniyah killing of one of their own.

Exhausted, Hussian reached the Samaneen Mosque
Where the men staggered in from a hard night's sleep
To do their ablutions and have a chance to meet
The Batiniyah Shaikh, Sharif Ali Vujoodi

The Samaneen Mosque. The end of morning prayers. WORSHIPPERS all wearing green turbans HUSSAIN is having difficulty identifying Shaikh SHAREEF ALI VUJOODI.

HUSSAIN: *(To a WORSHIPER in a green turban.)* Shareef Ali Vujoodi?

WORSHIPPER: No Sir.

HUSSAIN: Sorry, I thought you were Shareef Ali Vujoodi

Out of the melee of WORSHIPPERS SHAREEF ALI VUJOODI appears.

SHAREEF ALI VUJOODI: I am Shareef Ali Vujoodi.

HUSSAIN: *(Prostrating himself at his feet.)* As salamu aleiykum!

SHAREEF ALI VUJOODI: Waleiykum assalam.

HUSSAIN: Oh sir, I was told – but you all look the same–

SHAREEF ALI VUJOODI: You dare to insult me you unclean drop in the ocean of being!

HUSSAIN: I'm sorry, I didn't – I know that you're the only one who can help me get to paradise. I'm sorry –

SHAREEF ALI VUJOODI: How dare you presume to understand the secrets of the Un-present and of Heaven?

HUSSAIN: I don't. But you do, don't you? You are… I've been assured that 'you swim in the Ocean of Oneness and can help me navigate its choppy waters'.

SHAREEF ALI VUJOODI: Only if you have the fortitude?

HUSSAIN: Fortitude?

SHAREEF ALI VUJOODI: Courage.

HUSSAIN: If you knew what I'd been through you wouldn't be questioning my fortitude. I am prepared to alter the way I practise my faith to be with the one I love.

HUSSAIN stands up and they hug.

Trust me oh holy one, I've done everything that was expected of me.

SHAREEF ALI VUJOODI: I was there.

HUSSAIN: Sorry?

SHAREEF ALI VUJOODI: The Khurshah has intrusted his power to me. God is in my heart, and his light shines through my eyes. And in that light I can see those who desire nothing more than to be with him… wherever they happen to be.

HUSSAIN: Good, so I…, you know what I've been through.

SHAREEF ALI VUJOODI: Absolutely, but only when the soul controls your heart, body and mind, will you be allowed into Paradise.

HUSSAIN: Well I'm pretty sure mine does, doesn't it?

Pause.

SHAREEF ALI VUJOODI: Why did it take you so long to get here?

HUSSAIN: I wasn't aware that I had taken any longer than I needed to take.

SHAREEF ALI VUJOODI: And when you arrived on the West side of Mount Ararat and it still took you a day, a whole day to enter the cave.

HUSSAIN: Well, I didn't realize the place would be so busy, it was teeming with pilgrims. No one told me it was sacred to Christians and Jews as well us Muslims.

SHAREEF ALI VUJOODI: Your spiritual guide has never told you about the place where the prophet Abraham met God?

HUSSAIN: *(Slightly nervous.)* Well he might have done. He probably did. I'm not that religious – well, I am – it's just, like most people I guess, I only remember the bits I'm taught at the time they matter to me…

SHAREEF ALI VUJOODI: So most of your teaching has been a waste of time?

HUSSAIN: No, I was taught by my Uncle the great Imam Najamuddin Naishapuri.

SHAREEF ALI VUJOODI: Why should he be respected if you can't you can't remember half of what he has taught you?

HUSSAIN: I didn't say that.

SHAREEF ALI VUJOODI: Imam Najamuddin Naishapuri has been preaching against the Batiniyah faithful, forcefully. But you still think he's the best teacher.

HUSSAIN: The best teacher then but not now. Now he is second best. You are the best, because he definitely doesn't know how the living can get to paradise while they are still alive, if you know what I mean? Or if he does, he's never mentioned it.

SHAREEF ALI VUJOODI: Or you've forgotten.

HUSSAIN: I'm sure I would have remembered. If you can reunite me with Zamurrud while I'm still alive I'm sure you'll turn out to be the most devout man I've ever met. I'm sure you will. Have you been to paradise?

SHAREEF ALI VUJOODI: Yes.

HUSSAIN: It's remarkable. You've been to paradise and you've come back alive?

SHAREEF ALI VUJOODI: What else did your Najamuddin Naishapuri fail to tell you?

HUSSAIN: I don't know because I can't know what he hasn't told me, can I?

SHAREEF ALI VUJOODI: How do I know you are telling me the truth?

HUSSAIN: It's true. What do you think I should know that I don't know?

Pause

You'll help me find Zamurrud, won't you?

SHAREEF ALI VUJOODI: You must help yourself.

Silence.

Why did it take you three months to get to the crypt in Shahr-e-Kaheel?

HUSSAIN: It was difficult. The terrain. The diet. I was low on energy, and when I got there I had to get permission from this chief official who said unless I had something to give him he wasn't going to let me in, and because I hadn't any money, and I was loath to give away my shoes, I had to wait –

SHAREEF ALI VUJOODI: You sneaked in, in the early hours when he'd dozed off and no one was looking.

HUSSAIN: That's right. It was the only way. How did you know?

SHAREEF ALI VUJOODI: And because it was so dark you kept stumbling over people.

HUSSAIN: I didn't know whether they were dead or alive, but I wasn't going to be distracted. I found the prophets, as instructed. The two mummies lying in their glass coffins with their purple skins and sunken eyes, and I knelt between them as instructed.

SHAREEF ALI VUJOODI: And you were filled with dread and awe.

HUSSAIN: No, no, I was thinking about Zamurrud… Zamurrud, Zamurrud… Zamurrud on my mind. It was difficult not to feel scared especially when this shaft of dawn light shone through tiny slit in the ceiling and cuts across the two faces… suddenly they seemed to come alive. They were staring at me with their accusing eyes.

SHAREEF ALI VUJOODI: Accusing you of what?

HUSSAIN: Nothing. I don't know. Just accusing.

SHAREEF ALI VUJOODI: And try as hard as you could to focus on Zamurrud you couldn't.

HUSSAIN: I could. I love her more than life itself. I did as I was instructed.

SHAREEF ALI VUJOODI: You couldn't.

HUSSAIN: That's not true, I did. Honestly, I DID! How do you know what I was thinking.?

SHAREEF ALI VUJOODI: Then things got worse for you, didn't they?.

HUSSAIN: Did they?

SHAREEF ALI VUJOODI: I witnessed your helplessness –

HUSSAIN: What? When was I helpless? In what way? You mean when I tried to leave? You were there? I didn't see you.

SHAREEF ALI VUJOODI: I saw you.

HUSSAIN: How could you? When I tried to get out, and the keeper caught me? Not the chief, the official who I hadn't managed to bribe to let me in, in the first place… But how –

SHAREEF ALI VUJOODI: By God's light I saw what happened to you. You can't deny you weren't scared and ready to give up?

HUSSAIN: That's not true I wasn't frightened of the official. If I was frightened, it was because I thought I might die not having fulfilled the instructions in Zamurrud's letter. But as luck would have it, the corrupt chief, the keeper of the crypt, not the official but his boss had been assassinated that afternoon, by some of the Batiniyah sect –

SHAREEF ALI VUJOODI: At my instruction.

HUSSAIN: What? The town was on the brink of a civil war.

SHAREEF ALI VUJOODI: And that is when I sent my followers to support my spies and attack your captors, including the man you're talking about and that is how you managed to escape.

Pause.

If you want to see Zamurrud again, you will have to become one of us.

HUSSAIN: I thought that's what I was doing?

SHAREEF ALI VUJOODI: Do you believe that the truth is hidden, and can only be revealed to the uninitiated by those who know the reality?

HUSSAIN: I believe… Yes.

SHAREEF ALI VUJOODI: You must learn that the knowledge of God cannot be attained through anyone and everyone's reason and reflection but only through the teaching of our Khurshah, Imam Qayem Qayamat, lord of resurrection. Most of mankind is possessed of reason and everyone has views on the ways of religion. But, if the use of reason were sufficient for the knowledge of God, no sect could raise objections against other sects and all would be equal.

HUSSAIN: I suppose so.

SHAREEF ALI VUJOODI: It's a shame that people like you, you Sunnis –

HUSSAIN: I'll believe whoever I need to believe to be reunited with the one I love.

SHAREEF ALI VUJOODI: You Sunnis are prepared to listen to a host of doctrinal opinions about faith… and assume it is your prerogative to choose what suits. I must ask you where is the true faith in your Sunni contrary reasoning?

HUSSAIN: I don't know.

SHAREEF ALI VUJOODI: With your four schools of jurisprudence that differ in their interpretations of the Koran and application of religious law. Surely you must see, that in order that the people might be instructed and possessed of the true religion there needs to be a supreme religious authority on earth whose instructions are infallible. Someone who must be obeyed. Do you understand? Reason, my dear friend, is not sufficient.

HUSSAIN: Well, yes – but no – but yes if – No it's just that –

SHAREEF ALI VUJOODI: If you want to see your beloved again you must do what I say, and accept the Batiniyah faith as the one true faith.

HUSSAIN: Yes. Okay.

SHAREEF ALI VUJOODI: By giving his only daughter Fatima as wife to Ali, the Prophet, peace be upon him, designated Ali as his successor. You must accept that the prophet's father-

51

in-law, Abu Bhukar, had no right to assume the leadership of the faithful after the prophet died. Up until now you may have accepted the treacherous Abu Bhukar and the all false halifa that have followed him as the legitimate heir, you Sunnis with your black flag and your book of Sunna… but it's all lies. Poisonous lies. Our Shia flag is white, and the one who rules us is directly descended from Ali and Fatima, the Prophet's daughter. And the teachings of the Prophet, peace be upon him, find their most perfect expression in the doctrine of the Batiniyah. I repeat, if you want to see Zamurrud again you must be initiated into the faith… You must convert. Do you understand?

Pause.

HUSSAIN: Yes.

SHAREEF ALI VUJOODI: Sure.

HUSSAIN: I love her.

SHAREEF ALI VUJOODI: Don't ask me to let you see Zamurrud until the time is ready for you to see her.

HUSSAIN: I'm ready.

SHAREEF ALI VUJOODI: You will only be ready when you are resolved to devote your life to our cause.

Pause.

To do as I command you to do without hesitation.

Pause.

Believe me, obedience is not easy. The spirit of rebellion will rise in you as sure as any man. There will be times when your body will refuse to follow your will. And times when your reason will whisper a thousand reservations to your body. Resistance is the refrain of demons intent on turning you away from the true path of God. Do you understand?

HUSSAIN: If you'll let me.

SHAREEF ALI VUJOODI: I can't do anything until the strength of your resolve to commit to the one true faith has been put to the test.

HUSSAIN: But it has already, hasn't it? That's what my journey so far –

SHAREEF ALI VUJOODI: You must do as I command you to do.

HUSSAIN: All right. I am resolved. You know I am. I love Zamurrud. You know I do. With all my being I love her and want to be with her. We were betrothed. I will do as you command. As I have already done.

Pause

SHAREEF ALI VUJOODI: So, from now on don't desire to be with her, or say another word about her, until you are with her.

HUSSAIN: Sorry? I don't understand. For the past year I've been told to keep her in the forefront of my – Why?

SHAREEF ALI VUJOODI: The strength of your resolve can now only be measured by your commitment to me. Do, as I command you to.

You must now replace me for her in your thoughts… if you ever want to see her again.

HUSSAIN: But this is crazy.

SHAREEF ALI VUJOODI: It's perfectly straightforward, you must forget about her, and think only of me.

HUSSAIN: How can I?

SHAREEF ALI VUJOODI: Don't let reason stand in the way of paradise. You must carry out my commands, which are the true commandments of God. Work scrupulously and unquestioningly.

HUSSAIN: How? What do you want me to do?

SHAREEF ALI VUJOODI: Stop asking questions. / To me should obedience be rendered.

HUSSAIN: All right. No more questions

SHAREEF ALI VUJOODI: You will do everything I ask?

HUSSAIN: All right.

SHAREEF ALI VUJOODI: Good. Now listen… In life there are two realities, the reality of appearance, the outer, and the reality of the life within… the inner. We know we have a body which is how people recognise who we are, but we also have a heart that feels and a mind that thinks. The heart never lies but the mind tempers messages from the heart to protect it… and the body too come to that. Our bodies turn to dust but our thoughts and our feelings seek immortality, striving for significance until the end of time. You will remember when the prophet Kadhir killed a young boy for what seemed to his disciple Moses completely irrational reasons: – Kadhir explained to him, 'Because the child was destined to bring unhappiness to his parents'.

HUSSAIN: Forgive me but if you're going to ask me to do something sinful, something evil… I'm not sure that I can.

SHAREEF ALI VUJOODI: Don't you see, in your eyes that could happen, but in reality it couldn't.

HUSSAIN: I'm sorry I don't understand?

SHAREEF ALI VUJOODI: You presume – you unclean drop in the ocean of being! – to think that I will command you to do evil. That God is evil.

HUSSAIN: No, I don't. It's just the Batiniyah have a reputation. And you talk in riddles.

SHAREEF ALI VUJOODI: The story of Kadhir and Moses is clear, isn't it? Even if the act might seem evil to you the inner reality of the act, which only I will know, will be contained in the consequences, and they will be 'good'. I can assure you.

HUSSAIN: But surely the true consequences for me, of what I do, depend on my intentions. If I don't like what I'm being asked to do, then my intent in the doing is not good and the consequences would then be evil. Doesn't it say in the Koran, –

SHAREEF ALI VUJOODI: That doesn't make any sense and how dare you suggest my intent could be anything other than good!

HUSSAIN: I'm not saying yours would be evil. It's *my* intent I'm worried about, when I don't understand your intent. The true intent. According to the Koran, my soul will be blemished.

SHAREEF ALI VUJOODI: It's not me who talks in riddles it's you. Trust me. Parents will often punish a child for something its done wrong when the child will feel completely blameless. How many times do I have to tell you, the consequences aren't always immediately understood or appreciated? If you want to see Zamurrud in paradise you'd better do what I ask you to do, unquestioningly.

Pause

HUSSAIN: I am sorry master. I'm sorry if I ever doubted you… It won't happen again.

SHAREEF ALI VUJOODI: Hope springs eternal. You will stay here in the monastery with me, until you have clearly demonstrated your willingness and ability to commit to the Batiniyah faith and everything I ask of you, which is what God asks of you. Understood?

Pause

HUSSAIN: Understood.

SHAREEF ALI VUJOODI: You must subordinate your will to mine. And as my disciple you must replace Zamurrud's image with mine.

HUSSAIN: You said that, you said… and I will… I suppose… if I can? I can.

SHAREEF ALI VUJOODI: Even in the lonely hours of the night, in the solitude of your monastic cell which is where you will live while you are studying to become a true disciple of mine.

HUSSAIN: My will, will do that, will it? It will.

SHAREEF ALI VUJOODI: You will. Remember I am a man who has not only been to Paradise, but knows how to send others there. Also, it is within my power to summon the spirits of Paradise here.

HUSSAIN: Really? Do you mean to say, you could bring Zamurrud here? Master I didn't realize. Please!

SHAREEF ALI VUJOODI: The Khurshah as leader of the faith has bestowed this power on me and the Master of Cave. We are the only two who have the means.

You will see, I have disciples all over, and once a year they come back to this monastery to receive their instructions from me, as they do at Alamut to receive instruction from the Khurshah. Some of them travel long distances. You are joining their ranks. The more obedient to me and the Batiniyah cause, the further they progress on the road to salvation. The disciple is the sword, the hilt held by the master. It is the hand on the hilt that is culpable if there is anyone to blame.

SCENE SIX

Eleven months later SHAREEF ALI VUJOODI's disciples receive instructions from their Imam. One dies in the process. HUSSAIN accepts obedience is his password to paradise.

SHAREEF ALI VUJOODI: *(To a lone DISCIPLE.)* It is the responsibility of every human being to bear witness that there is no deity worthy of worship except Allah, and him alone.

Music. The room starts to fill with DISCIPLES. As they enter they announce where they are from.

DISCIPLE 1: Algeria.

DISCIPLE 2: Azerbaijan.

DISCIPLE 3: Kharakorum.

DISCIPLE 4: Arabia.

SHAREEF ALI VUJOODI: Ours is a holy war to advance
the caliphate. It is incumbent on all Muslims to pledge
allegiance to the caliph.

DISCIPLE 3: Oman.

HUSSAIN: Aamil.

DISCIPLE 4: Yemen.

DISCIPLE 2: Egypt.

DISCIPLE 1: Libya.

DISCIPLE 3: Zanzibar.

SHAREEF ALI VIJOODI: We know that in this world the
fulfilment of desire as well as Divine Will require that
the soul be severed from the body. If the soul becomes
dependent on things that give pleasure to the body – and
the body alone… then when the body dies the soul is lost
with it, hiding in the dust with nothing to sustain it but the
memories of past visceral pleasures that it is now denied.
Tortured it lives in a kind of hell. You, my dear disciples,
must learn, and some of you already know that there are
three stages to salvation. Firstly to minimize the reliance of
the soul on the corporeal we must – Anyone?

DISCIPLE 1: Not to let the soul govern everything your body
does. Sometimes let the body just do what it likes.

SHAREEF ALI VUJOODI: Correct. Secondly

DISCIPLE 4: In the same way that the body has time to itself so
must the soul. Give the soul time to itself.

SHAREEF ALI VUJOODI: Most of you have done this without
ever having to think about it. Through meditation,
devotion and obedience to me. It is the nature of your

vocation, and most of you are Already at the third stage far enough advanced on the path to salvation – to let your soul, whilst remaining in your body, visit the world of angels and the sphere of the Godhead, in the search of the secrets of the Light of All lights. If you die in this stage rest assured that as soon as your soul leaves your body it will be united with the Light of All Lights, The Being Who Has to Be and the Reason of All Reasons. But assuming you live, on your return from Paradise your soul will not achieve the sublime everlasting spiritual perfection it seeks whilst a prisoner in your body, suffering the trials of this world of four opposites.

DISCIPLE 2: *(To SHAREEF ALI.)* Master, as you can imagine, I don't understand how we're going to enjoy the pleasures of paradise when we haven't got a body?

SHAREEF ALI VUJOODI: Your soul may not have a body but it feels as if it had a body, because once it was within a body.

DISCIPLE 1: But without form how is it going to feel the pleasurable sensations we feel with our bodies? With seventy two houris on offer, whose virginity you say is miraculously re-established after every encounter, I'd hate to lose out –

SHAREEF ALI VUJOODI: Before entering the body the pure soul doesn't have the capacity to enjoy corporeal pleasure, you're right. But it is to learn those pleasures that it enters our bodies for the duration of our short lives. That is the purpose of life, to expose our souls to all kinds of intensely pleasurable and painful experiences, so that when we die and the soul leaves the body, it can adopt any shape it wants and can feel as it wants. Just as any one of you, passing through the stages of spiritual development taught here, can learn by stage three to make himself invisible, whilst remaining in his corporeal form. As I have done, on more than three occasions. And you can, in a state of ecstasy, in rapture, be disembodied. Agreed?

DISCIPLES: Agreed Master.

SHAREEF ALI VUJOODI: Likewise a well trained soul can manifest itself in any shape it wants to. Agreed?

DISCIPLES: Agreed.

DISCIPLE 3: Master, thank you for all the magnificent philosophical and spiritual secrets you have revealed to me. I have no doubt about anything you say, you're a man who has visited paradise many times and summoned its spirits. Now, please, send me there. I am an old man, my soul is ready, and I have done everything you have asked of me in this life. Send me because now my soul can learn nothing more from my body, it desires nothing more than to be released from the burden of the body.

Assisted by the other DISCIPLES, DISCIPLE 3 gets up and stands silently in the middle of the room. We hear his breathing. It is echoed by the others. Getting slower/ or faster and louder until there is one long, last exhalation. ALI VUJOODI hugs the DISCIPLE 3, collapses, and everyone in the room's forehead hits the carpet. After a few moments silence, a wailing starts, D3's body is wrapped in a white shroud and taken away.

HUSSAIN and SHAREEF ALI VUJOODI are left on their own.

HUSSAIN: *(Whispering.)* I have been with you for the past eleven months. I have served you with total obedience and unlimited veneration. All my thoughts start and finish with you. Surely, I am ready for paradise. If there is anything else you want me to do, tell me and I will do it immediately.

SHAREEF ALI VUJOODI: Remember that until your body can act independently of the soul you cannot proceed to the second stage of Oneness. You say you will do whatever I ask?

HUSSAIN: I vow.

SHAREEF ALI VUJOODI: Then kill Imam Najumuddin Naishapuri.

(Offering him a small dagger.)

I want you to go to Kabul, join his class again, and at the first opportunity you get – kill him.

HUSSAIN: My old spiritual leader?

SHAREEF ALI VUJOODI: Who has misled you for years.

HUSSAIN: My uncle?

SHAREEF ALI VUJOODI: Kill him.

Did you not swear –

HUSSAIN: I said after you he is the most erudite and god fearing man I have ever met...

SHAREEF ALI VUJOODI: Kill him.

HUSSAIN: But the Koran says 'The deliberate murder of a believer is an act of unbelief.'

SHAREEF ALI VUJOODI: Haven't you listened to anything I've said? 'You must let the body work independently of the soul.'

HUSSAIN: He's famed for his virtue. No living person can surpass him in learning! His interpretations of the book of Sunna, his disciples and his students lead large groups of Muslims throughout the Islamic world. Why?

SHAREEF ALI VUJOODI: No doubts or bad faith should defile your thinking if you want to get to paradise.

HUSSAIN: But what's he ever done to you?

SHAREEF ALI VUJOODI: I've already told you every overt act can have a covert aspect.

HUSSAIN: Why do you have to control what people believe? What does he preach that you are so afraid of? What privileges afforded to his followers are you denied? Religion was invented to bring us closer together not prise us apart. If you are prepared to look for it there's good in everyone. There's plenty of everything for everybody if only we could agree on the way to share it.

SHAREEF ALI VUJOODI: Shame on you that you have already forgotten Zamurrud's letter, 'If you love and desire me you

will serve and obey Shareef Ali Vujoodi until your purpose
is served.'

After awhile HUSSAIN takes the knife.

Music

SCENE SEVEN

HUSSAIN kills IMAM NAJAMUDDIN NAISHAPURI on his sick bed.

*A place of convalescence. Behind a wooden screen IMAM NAJAMUDDIN
sits in a large chair. A small table beside the chair with various remedies
for a fever. In front of the screen HUSSAIN.*

ATTENDANT 1: I'm sorry but 'no', you can't see him

HUSSAIN: Why?/ Is he ashamed of me for running away?

ATTENDANT 1: He's still feverous.

HUSSAIN: 'Allah is ever-pardoning,' he taught me that.

ATTENDANT 1: He's had it for three days and he fears he may
still be contagious.

HUSSAIN: He can't see a way to forgiving me, then I'm
without hope.

ATTENDANT 1: The Imam often speaks of you. How you were
his prize pupil and then –

HUSSAIN: I know, I know, I know, and it's all my fault, please
let me see him.

ATTENDANT 1: Maybe tomorrow. Maybe tomorrow, he'll feel
stronger.

HUSSAIN: I'm not frightened of catching whatever he's got. It
can't be worse than the pain of the shame I bare. Only his
forgiveness will stop me killing myself. Today, here, now.
Tell him for my own safety I can't leave without seeing
him.

IMAM NAJAMUDDIN: *(Calling from behind the screen.)* Hussain!

HUSSAIN: Uncle.

IMAM NAJAMUDDIN: Come here.

The screen is pulled back to reveal IMAM NAJAMUDDIN and ATTENDANT 2 in attendance. Both ATTENDANTS stand behind the Imam's chair, as HUSSAIN approaches his uncle.

HUSSAIN: God be with you, uncle.

IMAM NAJAMUDDIN: I'm disappointed in you Hussain.

HUSSAIN: Believe me Uncle, there was no evil intent, on our part. I was so in love with Zamurrud, I still am, I would have done anything for her, still will, and when she said, 'she wanted to do the Hajj and that she would marry me on the way to Mecca if I was prepared to go with her', I could see no shame in it. I didn't know what I know now, that her real purpose for leaving Aamil, and eloping with me was to find Musa's grave. He was murdered in the Valley of the Alburz, on the road to Qazvin.

IMAM NAJAMUDDIN: I remember that story.

HUSSAIN: And my beloved has met the same fate.

Beat.

IMAM NAJAMUDDIN: Zamurrud, dead?

HUSSAIN: Killed, like her brother before her, as she knelt by his grave and wept for the safe passage of his soul.

IMAM NAJAMUDDIN: And where were you?

HUSSAIN: Asleep, as Yakoob was when Musa was taken.

IMAM NAJAMUDDIN: By whom?

HUSSAIN: I don't know I didn't see. I'm telling you I was asleep and in the morning I woke up to discover her grave…

IMAM NAJAMUDDIN: Are you telling me the truth?

HUSSAIN: It's the truth. Believe me, Uncle it's the truth.

IMAM NAJAMUDDIN: In the province of the mind what we believe to be true either is true or becomes true because we need it to be true.

HUSSAIN: I'm not lying to you.

IMAM NAJAMUDDIN: Why are you telling me this?

HUSSAIN: I've come to ask for your forgiveness and for your help. It's nearly three years since Zamurrud died and I am still grieving for her, uncle. Grief like frost permeates every part of my being. I don't want to die but to forsake Aamil and spend the rest of my life in the pursuit of knowledge of the eternal Being until my soul can be reunited with hers. Your forgiveness will help me Uncle. Please protect me in the sanctuary of your home from those who will never believe or forgive me for the shame I have inflicted on my family. And accept the strength of the love I have for you and God, in my heart. Please lead my spirit to eternal peace, Uncle. Please let me join your class again and practise my faith faithfully?

IMAM NAJAMUDDIN: Reward and punishment are different names for the pleasure and pain our conscience inflicts on us as a consequence of what we do. Where is your conscience after what you have done?

HUSSAIN: In pain.

IMAM NAJAMUDDIN: Religious law as taught to every devout Muslim says 'to ignore your conscience is to sin, and to condemn yourself to hell.'

HUSSAIN: My conscience blames me for eloping with Zamurrud, but please by your forgiveness may I not end up in hell.

Pause.

IMAM NAJAMUDDIN: May Allah fulfil your desire, and one day bestow upon you the capability to succeed me in this school.

(To the ATTENDANTS.)

63

Fetch us some food and something to drink.

ATTENDANT 2: Oh Master, Master, Master!

ATTENDANT 1: Oh master you are feeling better!

ATTENDANTS leave.

IMAM NAJAMUDDIN: *(To HUSSAIN.)* Come here.

HUSSAIN doesn't move.

(Standing.)

Come here and give your uncle a hug.

Silence.

You're very quiet all of a sudden.

(Opening his arms.)

You can stay. Please stay. Don't worry, I believe you, nephew. I believe in you.

HUSSAIN hugs IMAM NAJAMUDDIN and stabs him to death. It is a ferocious attack, a brutal assassination.

ATTENDANT 1: He stabbed him twelve times.

ATTENDANT 2: After the seventh time. The knife appeared to linger in the body. Hussain twisted it…. and twisted it… Before pulling it out and stabbing him again, and again, and again, and again and again.

ATTENDANT 1: Before pulling it out and placing the warm wet blade on the quivering lips of the dying man. Then in one deft movement like a fisherman baiting a hook, he lifted out his tongue with the point of the knife, held it between finger and thumb, pulled it, and sliced it out. He sliced out the tongue that had preached to the faithful for so long.

ATTENDANT 2: Drilled the knife into his ears.

ATTENDANT 1: Gouged out his brain like a snail from a shell. And punctured his thinking with the point of the blade.

ATTENDANT 2: And slit his throat.

HUSSAIN turns, knife in hand, blood dripping, rooted to the spot.

HUSSAIN: What I did I didn't do. Shaikh Ali Vujoodi did this.

He can see good in this where I can see nothing but evil.

My Uncle trusted me, forgave me, paid me the highest respect and named me as his successor. What good can possibly come from what I have done? Whenever I look at these hands I will see his blood. No ocean can wash them clean...

(Drops the knife.)

It is my fate on the day of judgement to be poisoned by snakes, and burnt alive.

(Picking up the knife and momentarily looking like he's going to plunge the knife into his own chest.)

But to commit suicide is to meet the same fate.

(Letting the knife drop.)

All seeing, all knowing Shaikh Shareef Ali Vujoodi, you are my guide, if you can see inside my heart purify it, cleanse my thoughts. You said to think of you and, "be steadfast, knowing that in the Lord your labour is not in vain."

When I think of you... think of you... think of you what you can do... Doubts! Banish doubts. I have no doubts about what I have done!

I must trust you when you say a good I can't see and may never know will come of this.

For you are the most Holy of men, Shaikh Ali Vujoodi.

SCENE EIGHT

Overcome with grief, HUSSAIN is nevertheless rewarded for killing his spiritual leader.

SHAREEF ALI VUJOODI is doing his rosary. He discovers HUSSAIN in his cell. Before HUSSAIN has a chance to fall at his feet he is embraced by the Shaikh.

SHAREEF ALI VUJOODI: May the Eternal Light of Lights shine in you forever! Zamurrud can't wait to see you. She's so proud.

HUSSAIN: How can she be?

SHAREEF ALI VUJOODI: Because unlike you she can see beyond the present. She wants you to know, for what you've done, she loves you even more, than she ever did before.

HUSSAIN: *(Weeping.)* How can she? He was our spiritual leader. He put his trust in me and I in him.

SHAREEF ALI VUJOODI: Heed not the censures and denunciations of your heart. Banish conscience.

HUSSAIN: How? Why? Without conscience we are animals. And isn't the purpose of a conscience to integrate us with God, for he gave us his word, to help us know ourselves better, – to integrate us with each other, and to integrate us with ourselves.

SHAREEF ALI VUJOODI: You cannot cloak and confuse the truth with falsehood. Remember your spiritual prize for obeying me is Zamurrud's eternal embrace in Paradise.

HUSSAIN: Didn't Allah say to Ali, 'Believers are brethren, so make peace between your brethren'.

SHAREEF ALI VUJOODI: And to be reunited with the one you love in Paradise is proof positive you are a true Muslim. And so I say congratulations! You have reached the first step on the path to the Light of All Lights.

Silence.

ZAMURRUD: *(Off. Sings – pining, Zamurrud's Lament under the dialogue.)*

I'm Amethysts and pearls to you
Do everything you can
to join me here.

You're the reason I'm alive
I've no other reason
To survive.

In the shadows of the waterfall I see your face,
You're calling in the rustle of the leaves.

ZAMURRUD: *(Sings.)*

I pretend on silk soft cushions to be resting on your chest,
The sweet geraniums your body smell.

I dream of you beside me, but when waking you're not here,
I miss you more than life itself, my dear

I'm Amethysts and pearls to you
Do everything you can to join me here.

SHAREEF AL VUJOODI: Listen! Can you hear that? She is pining for you. First your body will be expected to act independently… and this it has done by killing Imam Najumuddin and now the soul must get its chance… and once you have mastered independence of your soul, inspired by the sight of paradise it will determine the way the body behaves… both working together for the greater good. As you will see them work in me. I trust you have the strength, courage and determination to complete your journey.

Use the faith you have to believe in Allah to believe what I say, that every overt act has a covert aspect.

Believe me, you've done a good deed. You won't ever have to repent for what you've done.

Pause

HUSSAIN: *(Calling out.)* Zamurrud! Zamurrud!

HUSSAIN grabs hold of SHAREEF ALI VUJOODI.

SHAREEF ALI VUJOODI: If you want to see her –

(Fetching a letter folded in the pages of a large book and giving it to HUSSAIN.)

Then take this letter to the northern gate of Isfahan, there you'll find a ruined mosque and outside the mosque a disciple of mine called Kazim Junoobi. A mendicant. When he's begging, which is whenever he's not praying, he makes this most extraordinary sound. So ugly you'll want to sew up his lips. You can't miss him. Give him this letter and whatever food you can.

KAZIM JUNOOBI enters, squats and howls for food.

KAZIM JUNOOBI: *(Howls for food.)*

SHAREEF hands HUSSAIN some food who hands it on to KAZIM. The howling stops. HUSSAIN gives him the letter.

SHAREEF ALI VUJOODI: On reading the letter he will take you to the Master of the Cave.

KAZIM JUNOOBI: *(Shouting into a cave.)*

O Master of the Cave! A firefly twinkles in the darkness of matter!

Lift the veil from the mirror that reflects the Radiances of the Godhead!

Oh Holy One, I have brought you a captive of the Four Opposites who is ready to learn the secrets of Paradise!

MASTER OF THE CAVE: *(Off. Echoey.)* Welcome Hussain! Come. Come and witness the miracles of divine power.

Blackout.

SCENE NINE

HUSSAIN visits paradise for the first time, and receives the mark of the HOURI.

In a dark cave.

HUSSAIN: *(In the darkness.)* Who are you?!

MASTER OF THE CAVE: Here!

HUSSAIN: Where?

Are you the Keeper of Paradise?

MASTER OF THE CAVE: *(Revealing himself.)* You can call me Master of the Cave, or the The Mount of Meaning.

HUSSAIN: That Moses met?

MASTER OF THE CAVE: *(Offering him another drink.)* The very same. Welcome Hussain!

HUSSAIN: You know my name.

MASTER OF THE CAVE: I know what you've been through these past three years and I also know a young houri who hasn't enjoyed her death without you ... Welcome to the Gateway to Paradise!

(Offering him a drink.)

Here, have some of wine and come and enjoy the pleasures of Paradise!

HUSSAIN: The last time I had a drink I lost Zamurrud, –

MASTER OF THE CAVE: That's her name, Zamurrud.

HUSSAIN: And now you're now encouraging me to drink to find her.

MASTER OF THE CAVE: The light and the shade! Four gardens, meticulously kept! Rivers of Milk, Water and Wine... Courtier angels and ravishing houris! Sights remarkable! I can't tell you the pleasure it affords me to be sending you to the Land of Light, into the arms of your true love... albeit temporarily.

HUSSAIN: What do you mean?

MASTER OF THE CAVE: Come on! Drink and you'll be with the angels before you know it.

HUSSAIN: What do you mean, temporarily?

MASTER OF THE CAVE: One stage at a time. The 'now' and then 'the then'.

HUSSAIN: *(Grabs the goblet and drinks.)*

MASTER OF THE CAVE: *(Revealing a mirror.)* Fix your eyes on the light reflected in this mirror and prepare to be transported.

HUSSAIN: *(Looking into a large mirror, full of reflected light.)* Paradise here I come!

The blinding bright lights of Paradise bleach the surroundings. The light then settles as a HOURIS chorus sing HUSSAIN a welcoming song.

HOURIS: *(Sing reprise of earlier song about Paradise.)*
Last night we dreamt of Paradise
Four rivers in gardens of light,
One for the spirit, the essence, the heart
One to rescue the soul.
Etc…

During the song the actors create the following stages of HUSSAIN's journey: HUSSAIN finds himself in a gold studded, gem encrusted rowing boat, rowed by beautiful rowers. He disembarks in a meadow of wondrous flowers, full of tuneful songbirds. Gold and silver divans rise out of the meadow. HOURIS everywhere and YOUNG MEN in an orgy of unbounded, unself-conscious pleasure.

HUSSAIN: No doubt about it. I have found the one true faith!

MARJAN drapes herself on HUSSAIN

Hello? We've met before?

MARJAN: By the canal. Marjan.

HUSSAIN: What are you doing here?

MARJAN: One day I fell into the water and drowned. We can do what we like now we're in Paradise.

HUSSAIN: I'm looking for Zamurrud.

MARJAN: It won't bother her, you know, if you want to enjoy me!

HUSSAIN: Do you know where she is?

Enter PARISA.

PARISA: Marjan! There's a a young hero wants a massage by the silver banyan.

MARJAN: Zamurrud's in the pearl pavilion with the Khurshah.

ZAMURRUD appears.

HUSSAIN: No she's not. She's here!

She looks at HUSSAIN. Their eyes meet.

Long silence.

Zamurrud!

ZAMURRUD: Hussain!

They hug.

PARISA: That's nice, eh?

ZAMURRUD: It's you.

HUSSAIN: It's you.

ZAMURRUD: Hussain.

HUSSAIN: Zamurrud.

PARISA: Parisa!

ZAMURRUD: Alive?

HUSSAIN: Unfortunately.

They hug again.

ZAMURRUD: Don't say that.

HUSSAIN: You feel as alive to me as you ever felt.

PARISA: She's dead.

ZAMURRUD: This is Paradise. My soul remembers how my body felt in your presence, and let's it feel it now.

HUSSAIN: *(Cries.)* Mine too.

ZAMURRUD: Don't cry! We're in the land of happiness!

HUSSAIN: *(To MARJAN.)* Would you mind? Thank you Marjan. Parisa…

MARJAN leaves. PARISA stays but at a further distance.

What happened?

ZAMURRUD: Somehow I made a martyr of myself. I hadn't intended to.

HUSSAIN: How?

ZAMURRUD: By grieving for Musa.

HUSSAIN: But who killed you?

PARISA: Avenging her death will not bring her back to earth.

HUSSAIN: I want to stay here for all eternity.

PARISA: It's not Zamurrud's fault that you're destined to live longer than her.

HUSSAIN: Please don't be angry with me… but if ever I needed proof of the one true faith this has got to be it.

You know, I've joined the Batiniyah.

ZAMURRUD: *(Starts to cry.)*

HUSSAIN: It was the only way I could get to see you before I die.

Theirs is the one true faith.

PARISA: You're in paradise. No one cries in Paradise.

HUSSAIN: Have you seen Musa?

ZAMURRUD: *(Whispers.)* No.

PARISA: There's no need to whisper. There are no secrets here. Paradise is a big place.

HUSSAIN: I'll help you find him.

PARISA: The light here is incredible, don't you think Everything with its own source – And the light itself is the source of its own light as though we were all both in and outside the sun.

HUSSAIN: What's she talking about?

PARISA: This is the divine light that Moses saw in the Valley of Aymen.

HUSSAIN: Really?

PARISA: This light is God. As described in the Koran.

HUSSAIN: God is glorious!

(Swinging her around and hugging her tight.)

Zamurrud, Zamurrud I love you!

ZAMURRUD appears unresponsive.

What 's wrong?

ZAMURRUD: I remember the last time you held me –

HUSSAIN: I'm never letting go. Never ever.

ZAMURRUD: But –

HUSSAIN: No buts.

ZAMURRUD: But –

HUSSAIN: What?

ZAMURRUD: You're going to have to leave.

HUSSAIN: Not before I've made love to you.

PARISA: She can't make love to you while you're still in your body.

HUSSAIN: You're happy enough for me to make love to Marjan. Why can't I make love to Zamurrud – we were going to one day. We were betrothed.

PARISA: You can't.

HUSSAIN: Why not? Has there been someone else?

PARISA: You can't stay here in the Realm of Light, while you're still capable of jealousy.

HUSSAIN: I can't wait to die. I'm ready to die. Please will somebody kill me!

PARISA: Strictly against the rules of paradise, I'm afraid. We'd risk banishment.

HUSSAIN: You mean I've got to return to earth and suffer –

PARISA: Like Jesus Christ. Yes.

HUSSAIN: What's Christ got to do with it?

ZAMURRUD: In the Koran.

HUSSAIN: I can't live without you.

ZAMURRUD: You've got to go.

HUSSAIN: *(Clasping her.)* You don't love me, do you?

ZAMURRUD: I do. I have been fated to deceive you, but we will soon be together again.

HUSSAIN: What are you saying? What have you done, Zamurrud? Zamurrud?

ZAMURRUD: Not what you're thinking. When you go back, thank everybody who helped you here and do whatever they ask of you, and soon we'll be together again. I promise.

PARISA: Zamurrud's right, you've got to live out the rest of your life appropriately, to come again and stay for ever.

ZAMURRUD: I will write to you.

Enter MARJAN.

MARJAN: He's done. Who's next.

PARISA: *(Consulting a list.)* Let me see.

ZAMURRUD: *(Still holding on to HUSSAIN, whispers.)* I'll write to you. I promise I will.

PARISA: You must come and walk the gardens, before you leave. Come on, Hussain!

MARJAN: Come! More wine!

PARISA: Come and sit on the thrones of light with us.

MARJAN: Or swim with me in the river of milk.

ZAMURRUD: Until we meet again!

HUSSAIN: Kiss?

They kiss. They are pulled apart by HOURIS and ZAMURRUD is led away. PARISA offers HUSSAIN.

MUSTAFA: *(Offering him a drink.)* Here, this'll make you feel better.

HUSSAIN: *(Drinks.)* Until the next time… my… darling.

MUSIC. HUSSAIN falls unconscious.

MARJAN returns and tries to whisper something in his ear. He doesn't reply. PARISA pulls her off him.

The KHURSHAH appears with MUSTAFA and a hot brand.

PARISA: Brand him!

MUSTAFA brands HUSSAIN's forehead.

HUSSAIN: *(Screams.)* KHURSHAH

Send him back.

SCENE TEN

HUSSAIN *learns if he wants to return to Paradise there's more killing to be done unless of course he can die in the process.*

The Mosque/ A sanctum within Alamut.

SHAIKH ALI VUJOODI and HUSSAIN in the Mosque.

SHAREEF ALI VUJOODI: Don't despair!

HUSSAIN: Why couldn't I stay?

SHAREEF ALI VUJOODI: Your corporeal desires cast a shadow on the light.

HUSSAIN: I don't see how. My intentions to Zamurrud are honourable, aren't they? And there was nothing about Paradise I would have ever wanted to change. And to see the Light of Lights – amazing – Please, sir there must be some way my soul can be liberated from my body sooner than the time I'm expected to die – whenever that is – without me having to kill myself.

SHAREEF ALI VUJOODI: There is. And I'm about to tell you how. Take this letter of recommendation to the Khurshah Imam Qayem Qayamat at Alamut. You have sworn allegiance to the Light of Lights and that Light is more brightly reflected in the Khurshah than any of us. He is the highest mediator between this world and the next. Making more visits between the two than any of us. Impress upon him, as I have done in the letter your steadfastness and obedience to our cause. And be prepared to do whatever he asks of you. Do so, and I have no doubt you will see your beloved Zamurrud sooner than death allows.

What's the matter?

Remember to whom you have sworn allegiance. And as your faith in our faith has grown so you have been entrusted with more secrets of the faith. Believe me, The Light of Lights shines more brightly in Imam Qayem Qaymet than in any other Muslim.

HUSSAIN: You said.

SHAREEF ALI VUJOODI: Ours is a holy war and you have a duty to kill the infidel. As you move ever closer to paradise for all eternity, the violence we inflict on the enemy must be steady and escalate. It is a strategy as revealed in the Koran. Random acts of violence are not enough. We must be consistently creative and shocking to assert the truth.

(Taking a mirror to show HUSSAIN his face.)

HUSSAIN: *(Rubbing his forehead.)* A scar. Like yours.

SHAREEF ALI VUJOODI: A houri's kiss.

(Showing him a similar.)

A mark of honour recognized by all mortals who've been to Paradise, and of course those who long to go…

You must be prepared to kiss the feet of Imam Qayem Qayamat. Who lives both in and beyond the material world.

HUSSAIN: I don't mind what you want me to do, but please let me die in the process.

SHAREEF ALI VUJOODI: Before you can meet Imam Qayem Qayamat you must go to Damascus and assassinate Imam Nasr Ibn Ahmed who has been preaching against us.

HUSSAIN: But he's like my Uncle. He's an inspiration to thousands and thousands of Muslims–

SHAREEF ALI VUJOODI: Cut out his tongue and crucify him. To teach his followers that the opportunities provided by God on earth are to be shared amongst more than the elite. Kill as many of his followers as stand in your way, and line the streets with their heads.

HUSSAIN: I've always believed God delivered us the Prophet, may he rest in peace to make us more merciful not brutal!

SHAREEF ALI VUJOODI: He delivered the prophet, may he rest in peace, to show us the truth about how we should live our lives! Stay steadfast, Hussain. Doubt not.

Paradise awaits you. If you're not in Alamut, by 27th day
of Ramadan then I'll assume you've given up any hope of
ever seeing Zamurrud again. The Imam Qayem Qayamet
will also be there on that day.

HUSSAIN: I thought Ramadan was the month of mercy.

SHAREEF ALI VUJOODI: And so it is.

SCENE ELEVEN

**Inside a glass pavilion in the castle of Alamut the true nature of
the Imam Qayem Qayamat is revealed.**

*Music. A room in a glass pavilion in Alamut. A troupe of HOURIS
dance and sing in front of The KHURSHAH and ZAMURRUD. They are
dismissed to reveal PARISA blindfolded and MUSTAFA.*

PARISA: How long am I supposed to wear this stupid blindfold?

KHURSHAH: Since everything I do would seem to inflame
your jealousy, I thought I'd spare you the pain of looking
at me.

PARISA: I've done everything you've ever asked of me. I've
fed you. Weeded your gardens. Sometimes slept with you.
In your thought-storms I've done my best to listen. I love
you.

KHURSHAH: When you were rescued you were offered
protection not love. How dare you abuse my generosity,
by insisting I reciprocate your overtures. You will not stir
my conscience to lie. I don't love. I will never love you.

PARISA: You need me.

KHURSHAH: You belong to me. Go and prepare the houris for
my brave followers, whilst I attend to Zamurrud. It is your
fault she doesn't love me.

*KHURSHAH waves his hand to MUSTAFA to dismiss PARISA and
bring in ZAMURRUD. A desolate ZAMURRUD stands apart.*

(To ZAMURRUD.)

My 'love' is like a goat. The older the teeth the younger the meat needs to be.

ZAMURRUD: *(Flinches.)* KHURSHAH

After everything I have given you, you could be a little more grateful. Observe the ways of the Prophet, and overcome all resistance in yourself.

After all this is paradise.

ZAMURRUD: This is hell more like.

Pause. He approaches ZAMURRUD and she freezes as he gently starts to caress her.

KHURSHAH: Really there is nothing to distinguish between my beautiful gardens and paradise. Ask Musa, if you don't believe me.

ZAMURRUD: If I could find him.

KHURSHAH: If I wasn't so in love with you I'd rape you, and stone you for betraying your beloved.

ZAMURRUD: Please let my brother is in the real paradise.

KHURSHAH: One day, after my devotions I fell into a deep sleep and God's messenger appeared to me in a dream and led me through the seven heavens to Paradise and the throne of God. And there in the brilliant light of Allah, he said to me, Imam Qayem Qayamat, from now on you are my representative on earth, take a good look at these gardens and then return to earth and build an exact replica within Alamut and gather the most beautiful men and women you can find, and instruct them in the faith and command them to behave as houris, and then... invite those enlightened heroes who have fought and will continue to fight for the just cause of the one true faith, to enjoy them... And let your houris ravishing bodies, their wine, and their song be our heroes' aspiration and reward.

ZAMURRUD: You trick those young men into risking their lives to kill for you, as you are doing to Hussain.

KHURSHAH: Allah said to me, 'only you and the Prophet,' may he rest in peace, 'have been afforded the privilege of crossing into the real paradise while you are still alive, but our young heroes will not feel cheated if you do a good job and make them believe your gardens are the real thing. Believe me, they should know what joys will be offered to them for all Eternity for doing the work of God.'

My devotees are promised the heaven they have seen and tasted, that is why they are so brave: that is why they think themselves invincible: that is why many long for their death and are afraid of nothing. They trust me. And this Paradise.

KHURSHAH places his hand between her thighs.

Are you a virgin?

ZAMURRUD: Doesn't the Koran say the maidens in paradise should stay virgins forever?

KHURSHAH: It's true. That is why no man who has ever visited my gardens has questioned a houri's virginity. Parisa's got these powders. Good enough to fool a beginner.

But don't worry, when you lose yours it'll be to me and then you'll be my wife. Do you love me? Do you?

ZAMURRUD: Please just kill me, like you killed my brother.

KHURSHAH: Tell me how much you love me and then let me make love to you.

ZAMURRUD: No.

KHURSHAH: If you want to know the truth about what happened to your brother.

Love?

One kiss?

After a long silence, ZAMURRUD kisses him on the cheek.

Our quest for pleasure is the purpose of life. Our senses feed and monitor our brains.

ZAMURRUD: What did you do to Musa?

KHURSHAH: Kiss me again?

ZAMURRUD: Did you kill him?

KHURSHAH: *(Starting to ravish her.)* Let me dote on you... kiss and freely fondle your firm, fresh, flesh... to think...

ZAMURRUD: Did you?

KHURSHAH: Love me.

You will love if you want me to be honest with you.

ZAMURRUD bites him and he breaks away.

ZAMURRUD: I have made a vow to Hussain!

KHURSHAH: Damn Hussain! He doesn't care for you!!/ He has renounced his love for you!

ZAMURRUD: How can I possibly love you? You've killed my brother, kept me a prisoner in a fake paradise and deceived the man I love into doing the most brutal acts imaginable in the name of God. I can't love you! I will love you!

KHURSHAH: Listen, what's wrong if my power is predicated on my ability to deceive? Whose isn't? There isn't a ruler in the world who doesn't lie for the sake of the people. There isn't a faith that doesn't deceive its many followers...

Look, we are born we don't know why. And we die none the wiser. And in the face of such uncertainty we muddle through trying to ignore the fear we have, that what we do and who we are amounts to nothing. Dust in the universe.

If this is the case, you think, why don't we end it? Why do we go on subjecting generation after generation to this fear.

Why? Why, my darling Zamurrud?

(Seducing her with his tongue.)

Because occasionally, like the sun bursting through the clouds... the sight of something beautiful or a kind gesture, the feel of another body, the meeting of minds... these things impact upon our senses so profoundly, our senses are sent to defeat our reason... immediately ...to dispel all fear and hopelessness. Throughout our short lives under sporadic attack from our senses our treacherous brains work tirelessly to invent meaning... any meaning, any reason ... because if life can make me feel like this, wonderful, magical, eternal, then there must something out there, bigger than us, a force bigger than the universe to help sustain the ecstasy of life, the unadulterated pleasure, the wonder, the joy and happiness I'm feeling...being alive in your presence!

We can't be blamed for taking comfort in the lies of faith. We need fairy tales.

KHURSHAH approaches ZAMURRUD and starts to undress her

The Shiites and the Sunnis defend their different truths, Christians of all sects, Jews, Brahmins, Buddhists, fire worshippers, pagans all passionate about what they believe. Because all humanity is entangled in ignorance, all are subject to fabrications and lies. Until the dead return to tell us otherwise.

What does it matter which makes the most sense? Let the one who makes the most sense at any given time be rewarded for doing so.

But in the face of death I fear sense makes no sense at all. So therefore...

If all we can ever know is nothing then I can do what I want, and you can, with a free conscience do my will.

(Grabbing her by the neck.)

Now, don't bite me. Kiss me you dog!

SCENE TWELVE

The brutal killing of Nasr Ibn Ahmed.

To the sweetest music. The FOLLOWERS of NASR IBN AHMED at prayer. They are joined by HUSSAIN. They leave to allow the Imam to offer tahajjjud (his night prayers.) Alone in a mosque, HUSSAIN emerges out of the darkness to crucify him and cut out his tongue.

FOLLOWER: He pulled back his head.

FOLLOWERS: Ahhh!

FOLLOWER 2: He placed the blade on his neck.

FOLLOWERS: Cut!

FOLLOWER 3: The blood gushed.

FOLLOWERS: Slice!

FOLLOWER: The breath groaned –

FOLLOWERS: Death.

SCENE THIRTEEN

The devoted followers of Imam Qayem Qayamet having assassinated any number of political enemies make their claims to visit paradise again before dying. Hussain is forced to wait his turn/...

Alamut. FIDAYEES (devoted followers of the imam.) surround KHURSHAH.

KHURSHAH: Well done, well done! But none of your assassinations beats what you did to Genghis Kahn's cousin Chughtai Khan. Remind us how you inveigled yourself into his company and waited for the perfect moment.

DEEDAR: *(To KHURSHAH.)* It wasn't easy. As you can imagine, the cousin of Chengis Khan is a big man, and I'm not, and like all Mongol leaders strong as a wall. And as you can imagine, I thought I'd never find a moment to kill Chughtai because he was always surrounded by body guards and followers, but I did, I found my moment to get him by making a friend of his son Manku Kahn, Gengis' nephew. And we got on very well, and as you can imagine, he started to rely on me for companionship because, I'm a bit of a clown, and I made him laugh. You see and it wasn't long before Manku Kahn introduced me to his father, and as you can imagine… I'm very sociable… and well, we all got on very well… And then they invited me to stay with them –

Enter HUSSAIN prostrate in front of KHURSHAH.

HUSSAIN: This is my Imam. This is my Imam.

TWO FOLLOWERS step forward and lift HUSSAIN up.

FOLLOWER: Who are you? What do you want?

Passing VUJOODI's letter to a FOLLOWER who in turn passes it to KHURSHAH.

HUSSAIN: Hussain. Sheik Vujoodi sent me. Oh, Imam Qayem Qayamat, I've come because I want to see Paradise again.

FOLLOWER: I'm sure you do, young man but like everybody else here, you must wait your turn.

KHURSHAH: *(Whilst reading HUSSAIN's letter.)* Deedar continue.

DEEDAR: And then one day, I should say night, when Manku was away – he'd gone to meet Halaku Kahn who'd just come back from ransacking some place or other, I managed to tie up Chuhtai – that's the father of the nephew, are you with me? – while he was asleep, and as you can imagine I just plunged this golden dagger into his heart.

HUSSAIN: I've killed two important men to get here. Imam Najumuddin Naishapuri and –

FOLLOWER: You must wait your turn.

KHURSHAH: So in the end, you managed it, you killed him?

HUSSAIN: Yes, and Imam Nasr ibn Ahmad. I'm definitely deserving of another trip to paradise immediately.

KHURSHAH: I wasn't talking to you

(Gesturing DEEDAR to continue.)

Deedar…

DEEDAR: He writhed and moaned as the blood oozed from his massive chest, and his eyeballs rolled up into his head, turning their sockets white, and blind… lest they should witness how deliberately I twisted and turned the knife in his flesh. Spared the sight of my hatred.

KHURSHAH: My brave, little Deedar.

DEEDAR: I killed him. I butchered him.

Applause.

KHURSHAH: And you let his followers know why you'd done it?

DEEDAR: I left a note for his daughter, Princess Balghan Khatoon, explaining everything.

KHURSHAH: By all reports a formidable woman.

DEEDAR: More of a letter than note, more of a book than a letter. I gave it to her in the dark so she didn't see me. That was a tough assignment, Master. It took me much longer than expected. But my trusty dagger has never missed its mark. I so want to see paradise again as soon as possible. / I had such a great time there. Any chance?

HUSSAIN: That makes two of us.

FOLLOWER: Three of us.

HUSSAIN: I'm coming with you. / Zamurrud's waiting for me.

KHURSHAH: Not yet, you're not.

FOLLOWER: You'll be lucky, you've only just arrived. You can't expect the Imam to intercede for you without having done anything.

HUSSAIN: What do you mean? I've killed / two men for her.

FOLLOWER: Two? We've all killed more than that

HUSSAIN: Two important men.

KHURSHAH: In the words of God to Moses, Hussain, the Light of Lights is not yet ready to welcome you to paradise –

85

HUSSAIN: Why? What d'you mean? My betrothed is waiting for me.

KHURSHAH: Is she still?

HUSSAIN: How much more killing have I got to do to prove to you I'm worthy of a second visit?

FOLLOWER: Show some respect!

KHURSHAH: *(Folding up the letter.)* Your master who sent you extols your learning, your courage and your bravery –

HUSSAIN: And I never disobeyed him. Come on, Zamurrud's waiting –

KHURSHAH: …Extols your courage and bravery but not your honesty –

HUSSAIN: I'm an honest man.

KHURSHAH: Is Zamurrud a virgin?

HUSSAIN: What's it to you?

KHURSHAH: Is she?

HUSSAIN: Yes, of course she is. We never had the chance to get married.

KHURSHAH: *(Reading again.)* Extols your honesty your courage and bravery but not your patience.

HUSSAIN: My patience?

Alright, alright, I'm being patient…

I'm patient…

I'm ready when you're ready.

KHURSHAH: So Deedar, you've completed the task assigned to you –

HUSSAIN: Assign me another task, then. Go on..

KHURSHAH: Jalal-ad-Din is dead.

HUSSAIN: I'll do anything. Anything you ask.

KHURSHAH: *(To DEEDAR.)* You'll visit paradise today.

DEEDAR: *(Hardly able to contain his joy.)* Allah-hu-Akbr

HUSSAIN: And me!

KHURSHAH: No.

HUSSAIN: No?

KHURSHAH: No.

HUSSAIN: Why? I'll do anything you want me to. Who do you want me to kill? I don't care, I'll kill you if you want me to.

(Getting physical with KHURSHAH whose followers restrain HUSSAIN.)

I've already killed two of the most devout men on the planet! Why not a third!

The FOLLOWERS rush to defend their Imam.

KHURSHAH: *(To his FOLLOWERS.)* Out! Take him out of here! She doesn't love you!

HUSSAIN: What did you say?

KHURSHAH: Zamarrud, doesn't love you. She loves me.

Silence.

HUSSAIN: No.

KHURSHAH: I have enjoyed her body and soul and she never wants to set eyes on you again.

HUSSAIN: *(Desperately trying to grab at the daggers of the FOLLOWERS.)*
Kill me then! Come on then, kill me! Come all you brave assassins, assassinate me! One of you! Kill me! All of you! KILL ME!

KHURSHAH: STOP!

FOLLOWERS throw HUSSAIN to the ground.

AIthough the wretch deserves to die his soul doesn't deserve martyrdom. Chuck him out with the babies. Let the vultures pick at him. Let his soul be lost to the winds.

HUSSAIN: No, no. Not my soul. I'm sorry. Imam Qayem Qayamat! Forgive me. Sorry, sorry, sorry! Forgive! Please Forgive me! My desire, my passion, my love, my jealousy raged my senses senseless. I'm tired. I'm fearful. I'm faithful. I'm sorry. Please let me, poor lowly devotee stay to do your bidding. I know you were testing me… my body …Please –

KHURSHAH: Out.

HUSSAIN: What ever you want. Ask of me.

I'll do anything.

HUSSAIN is led away. MUSIC. Followed by KHURSHAH. Some FOLLOWERS stay behind.

FOLLOWER: Do you know what?

FOLLOWER 2: What?

FOLLOWER: The last time I went to paradise, one desire I had remained unfulfilled.

FOLLOWER 2: *(Surprised.)* Really?

FOLLOWER: Yes. There was this beautiful woman I met there.

FOLLOWER 2: Only one.

FOLLOWER: She didn't respond to anything I said or tried to do to her.

FOLLOWER 2: Hardly paradise for you then.

FOLLOWER 3: Same happened to me.

FOLLOWER: What did she look like?

FOLLOWER 3: I talked to the Khurshah about it and he said, 'as a mortal being visiting paradise, you carry with you lots of profanities and impure thoughts. And you've got to remember that you're not experiencing paradise, in the same holy and spiritual way that your soul will when the time comes.' He claimed to have made love to her.

FOLLOWER 2: I know the one you mean – beautiful but totally unresponsive. I was told by Khurshah the last time I went, to avoid her or I'd never visit paradise again. It seemed like he was jealous. Another Houri told me she was dangerous because apparently, although she'd been there a long time, she was still connected in some bizarre way with the material world and a man called Hussain.

FOLLOWER: That was Hussain. Her name is Zamurrud. Wait till she hears the vultures have picked his body to pieces, and his soul has been lost in the wind.

SCENE FOURTEEN

Since Khurshah's rejection of her, Parisa has had second thoughts about Paradise. The Houris write to the Princess Balghan Khatoon

MARJAN: All your life you have been a prisoner, Parisa. What Zamurrud is saying, is if we can get another letter to Hussain, we can tell him to take this letter to Princess Balghan Khatoon, who is still, four years after the event – if the disciples are to believed – mourning the assassination of her father.

PARISA: But why two letters? Why can't he just tell her the plan and come?

ZAMURRUD: In my letter to the Princess, which I have instructed him not to read –

PARISA: But why?

MARJAN: She'll suspect his motives, won't she?

ZAMURRUD: *(Holding up the letter to the Princess.)* I've explained the truth of our situation and his. He will have to answer truthfully when she cross examines him. If he is honest and our versions of the truth concur then we can count on her support.

PARISA: But Hussain still believes we're in Paradise?

MARJAN: That's the point.

PARISA: Why don't we just tell him?

ZAMURRUD: Trust me, I know what I'm doing.

MARJAN: There's a chance, given their hatred of the Batiniyah and her desire to prove that women are as brave as men, that she will be sympathetic to our cause and with our knowledge of how to get into the castle undetected, lead a campaign against Alamut herself to kill Deedar, the Khurshah and all his followers and rescue us.

What if she can't read?

ZAMURRUD: My father told me that unlike common Mongol women she's educated, sophisticated and even has a passion for Persian poetry. How will we get it to him?

MARJAN: When I take out the babies –

ZAMURRUD: What about Mustafa?

PARISA: I'll deal with him.

MARJAN: What if Hussain isn't strong enough?

ZAMURRUD: When he reads there's no such place as Paradise and we're all prisoners here in Alamut, he'll be plenty strong enough.

SCENE FIFTEEN

On a wretched mountainside HUSSAIN is close to despair when he is rescued by a dream.

HUSSAIN is discovered on the mountainside. The shadows of buzzards sweep the ground. Enter the ghost of MUSA.

HUSSAIN: *(Bound, half asleep, dreaming.)*

Musa?

MUSA: How is my sister?

HUSSAIN: Who killed you?

MUSA: We were resting in the field, when we were ambushed by a flock of fairies who poured out of the mountains –

HUSSAIN: But they weren't real fairies, were they?

MUSA: No, not real fairies, but a horde of houri slaves set free to do their ablutions by the canal. We shared their food and wine and they showed us a good time –

HUSSAIN: I didn't know you drank wine.

MUSA: At a given signal they were driven back into the mountain by an army of Batiniyah thieves who stole everything we had. I did what I could to defend myself but there were too many, and one with jade eyes slit my throat as though he was bleeding a goat. Yakoob was lucky he had drunk himself into a stupor and fainted and they left him for dead.

HUSSAIN: Where are you now?

MUSA: In paradise.

HUSSAIN: I'm sorry to have missed you.

MUSA: Where's Zamurrud?

HUSSAIN: She's with you, isn't she?

MUSA: No.

HUSSAIN: She's waiting for me but I can't seem to die fast enough. And I'm worried that after everything I've done I'm likely to be heading for hell. What do you mean, haven't you met yet?

MUSA: We design and plant gardens, but I am in the garden of all gardens. The garden within me, where ever-flowing waters purify my soul... That's where you'll find me on the day of judgement.

HUSSAIN: What do you mean?

Enter MARJAN with a basket of embryos.

What do you mean?

MARJAN: Still alive?

HUSSAIN: Musa!

MUSA disappears.

MARJAN: Here, let me free you.

HUSSAIN: Am I dead? / Am I in paradise

MARJAN: You can't before you've freed us. Here's a letter for you?

HUSSAIN: Who from?

MARJAN: Zamurrud.

HUSSAIN: Another one.

MARJAN: Zamurrud was neither killed nor martyred. The paradise you visited is an artificial one, created by the Khurshah to deceive his followers into doing his political bidding. We are prisoners there. Everything that has happened is the consequence of her helplessness and your gullibility. Read this letter if you don't believe me. How can you possibly ever have thought you had left this world and entered another. Who has ever returned from dead?

MUSTAFA: *(Off.)* Marjan!

MARJAN: Coming! Zamurrud's letter will explain everything. Don't open the letter to Princess Balghan Khatoon just take it to her.

HUSSAIN: Princess Balghan? But –

MARJAN: Know you are who you need to be when you need to be that person.

HUSSAIN: What?

MARJAN: That person still wants to marry Zamurrud, doesn't he? That person still wants to do the Hajj.

HUSSAIN: Yes.

MUSTAFA: *(Off.)* Marjan! Is he dead yet? The Khurshah is waiting.

MARJAN: No he's not dead. The vultures don't like the meat.

MUSTAFA: Shall I kill him myself?

MARJAN: I'll do it. Do what the letter –

HUSSAIN: But the last time.

MARJAN: *(To MUSTAFA.)* He's dead.

(To HUSSAIN.)

Go on.

MARJAN frees HUSSAIN who reads the letter.

SCENE SIXTEEN

Princess Balghan receives Hussain in her garden.

The Princess' garden.

PRINCESS: 'In this letter your betrothed presumes I am grieving for my father, as much as she grieves for her brother, Musa'.

HUSSAIN: She would never have been kidnapped if she hadn't insisted on finding his grave. And I would never have had to convert if I hadn't wanted to be with her for the rest of my life, to help her get over her grief.

PRINCESS: She says, 'my father was assassinated by a Batiniyah Disciple killer, called Deedar, and he is in Alamut.'

HUSSAIN: That's true.

PRINCESS: She's asking me to raise an army and eradicate a great evil from the face of the earth, and to rescue the women captives. Are you Batiniyah?

HUSSAIN: Yes.

PRINCESS: Have you been to paradise?

HUSSAIN: Yes. But it wasn't a real paradise, and I had to kill two people I respected most in the world to get there. If I wanted to see Zamurrud again I had to…do as the

Khurshah commanded... I was told it was arrogant of me to assume I could predict the consequences of my actions and I should stop trying to distinguish between good and bad –

PRINCESS: So if the Khurshah had said jump, you would've jumped?

HUSSAIN: Yes

PRINCESS: If you were asked to kill again, would you?

HUSSAIN: That would depend on who was doing the asking and the consequences

PRINCESS: And who would decide the consequences?

HUSSAIN: Me. My conscience.

PRINCESS: And what dictates your conscience?

HUSSAIN: Love.

PRINCESS: But hasn't your love for Zamurrud been the reason you've embraced so much evil?

HUSSAIN: Yes.

PRINCESS: So what is going to determine your conscience from now?

HUSSAIN: I don't know.

PRINCESS: Your intelligence.

HUSSAIN: I don't know what I believe any more.

PRINCESS: I would suggest you believe what you have believe as long as your faith doesn't harm anyone else's. My Uncle, Ghengis Kahn always said, his success as a ruler was predicated on religious toleration. There are prophets who are worshipped and to whom everybody does reverence. The Christians say their God was Jesus Christ; the Saracens, Mohammed; the Jews, Moses; and the idolaters, Budhists Borhan; and I do honour and revere all four, and nature, to the mountain and the winds. Come on you fool. Zamurrud's letter says you are to lead me to her grave, and from there she has suggested how we should enter the castle via a cave where she will meet us, and identify my father's assassin. I can't wait to throw his heart to the dogs. In two days' time my cousin Manku Kahn is leading an army of forty thousand to punish the caliph of Baghdad. I'll ask him to divert five hundred men to accompany our mission. There is nothing a Mongolian warrior likes more than to kill an old adversary.

SCENE SEVENTEEN

ALAMUT is ransacked.

The PRINCESS, HUSSAIN and a MONGOL SOLDIER enter.

PRINCESS: Shh! Is this her grave?

HUSSAIN: Yes.

PRINCESS: Then, at the foot of the hill over, there's the entrance to a cave.

HUSSAIN: Really?

PRINCESS: That's what the letter says.

They walk on and enter the cave.

There should be a bundle here somewhere…

MONGOL: Here. Dresses.

PRINCESS: We're to enter the castle disguised as houris.

HUSSAIN: They'd better fit.

As they are getting dressed enter MUSTAFA.

MUSTAFA: Who's there?! Is that you? Show your face you stupid bitch! /Zamurrud!

HUSSAIN: *(Whispers.)* If my voice sounds unfamiliar it's because I have cried myself hoarse.

MUSTAFA: The luckiest whore in Alamut and you persist in trying to escape.

HUSSAIN attacks MUSTAFA

Ahh!

HUSSAIN attacks him and kills him.

ZAMURRUD: *(Calling in a whisper.)* Who's there?

HUSSAIN: Zamurrud?

(Calling.)

Zamurrud!

ZAMURRUD: Hussain?

ZAMURRUD appears out of the darkness. Seeing HUSSAIN they hug.

PRINCESS: Later!

ZAMURRUD goes to hug PRINCESS.

MONGOL: Later!

HUSSAIN: *(Introducing the PRINCESS.)* And this is Princess
    Balghan Khatoon.

PRINCESS: Where's the Batiniyah disciple who killed my
    father?

ZAMURRUD: He'll be in the courtyard listening to the
    Khurshah, with all the other disciples, messengers and
    missionaries.

PRINCESS: I've got an army of five hundred standing by to
    ransack the place. If we're to be successful we'll need to
    surprise them, which will be impossible if impossible if this
    underground passage is the only way –

ZAMUURUD: No, no. Where are they?

PRINCESS: At the crossroads on the hill –

ZAMARRUD: Then they can cross the bridge by the canal.
    There's a path on the other side. If we attack from within,
    they can block their escape route.

PRINCESS: Deedar is mine.

ZAMURRUD: Others didn't believe me but I knew you'd
    come.

MONGOL: Will we get to see fake paradise?

ZAMURRUD: Follow me. Quietly.

> *KURSHAH is in the courtyard. ALI VUJOODI, MASTER OF THE CAVE, DEEDAR in attendance. The sound of a throng of people.*

MONGOLS: *(Sing.)* We fight side by side
    For what is right!
    It is our destiny
    To crush the enemy
    And seal a great
    Mongolian victory!

KHURSHAH: All praise is due to Allah. We praise him. We seek his aid, and ask for his forgiveness. We seek refuge from Allah from wickedness. From any evil in our souls. Whomsoever Allah guides then none can misguide him; and whomsoever Allah lets stray none can guide him back. There is no God but Allah alone, and Mohammed, may the blessings and peace of Allah be upon him, is his slave and messenger.

> *Enter PRINCESS followed by MARJAN, PARISA, ZAMURRUD and HUSSAIN. Under the KHURSHAH's speech.*

MARJAN: He'll be here somewhere.

PRINCESS: Is that him?

ZAMURRUD: No. That's the Master of the Cave. A dog!

MARJAN: Let me kill him.

ZAMURRUD: /Paradise is not a house for men only.

PRINCESS: Go on then.

ZAMURRUD: Allah looks at our hearts and deeds not our bodies. Let me.

MARJAN: Me.

PRINCESS: Me.

MARJAN: Oh Master of the cave, do you like riddles?

MASTER OF THE CAVE: Yes, you know I do?

MARJAN: Then answer me this one? I start with a 'v' and every women has one, and with it she will get what she wants?

MASTER OF THE CAVE: I know, I know.

PRINCESS: A voice.

PARISA: That's not what you were going to say. Is it, you pillock?

PRINCESS: Kill him!

MARJAN and PARISA kill the MASTER OF THE CAVE.

KURSHAH: We fight in obedience to Allah, and as a means of coming closer to him. We fight because He – the Glorified commanded us to fight.

ZAMURRUD: There that's him.

PRINCESS: Deedar?

DEEDAR: Yes.

PRINCESS kills DEEDAR.

PRINCESS: Who's next?

KURSHAH: Allah the exalted says, 'he who fights in the cause of Allah and is killed or achieves. We will bestow upon him a great reward.' It is beholden upon us to fight and be patient, and upon Allah is the victory. We should not let the mobilization of forces against us alarm us, frighten us or break our resolve, for we will be victorious with Allah's power and strength.

HUSSAIN: Shareef Al Vujoodi!

PARISA: And then that sanctimonious unctuous toad, the Khurshah let him choke on his own lies.

MARJAN: Shaping the word of the God to suit his devious purposes. There is no evil more evil than what he has done to our faith.

PRINCESS: Words are the root of all misunderstandings.

KURSHAH: Do not be amazed. Rejoice in the contract you have made.

HUSSAIN attacks ALI VUJOODI.

SHAREEF ALI VUJOODI: Mercy! Mercy! Have mercy on my helplessness. Mercy on you. Sometimes I sit on a lofty tower. Sometimes I stare at the sole of my foot.

HUSSAIN: All the souls of your victims are in the blade.

HUSSAIN kills ALI VUJOODI.

KURSHAH: And if we are afflicted with killing and our wounds become many, and the storms rage against us, and our adversaries become great, it will come as no surprise. It is Allah's promise to us to persist in face of adversity, and our triumph too will come as no surprise.

ZAMURRUD, HUSSAIN and MARJAN.

ZAMURRUD: Behead him.

PRINCESS: Exile.

MARJAN: But after all that he – He's the one that started it all.

PRINCESS: Each of us is more than the worse thing we have ever done. Take him away. Far away. Somewhere where there are no Batiniyah where he can ruminate on his fate. Then set Alamut on fire. You are free!

MONGOLS sing their victory song.

MONGOLS: Swords in our hands
 We kill each and every man
 Victory songs telling
 Of our might!
 Arrows are raining
 Down on our enemy
 We fight side by side
 For what is right!
 It is our destiny
 To crush the enemy

And seal a great
Mongolian victory

Music.

ZAMURRUD: Thank you Princess.

HUSSAIN: Thank you.

ZAMURRUD: We must pray for forgiveness.

HUSSAIN: For what?

ZAMURRUD: For the deaths we have caused in the name of love. I should never tried to persuade you to rescue me. You would never have had to –

HUSSAIN: You can't blame yourself I was the one who killed my uncle. We'll do Hajj.

You still want to, don't you?

And we'll get married on the way.

PRINCESS: Having revenged the death of Chughtai, it would make me brim with happiness to see you fulfil your desires for each another. Get married, and bear the shame of returning to Aamil, come and live with me.

HUSSAIN: In the eyes of God I understand Zamurrud we are both guilty of killing innocent people, but I was deceived and you were a prisoner. Allah is most gracious, Allah is most merciful.
Well?
You've always been rubies and coral to me! Amethysts and pearls. Will you marry me?

MONGOLS: It is our destiny
To crush the enemy
And seal a great
Mongolian victory

THE END